Peter Sherran

D1368866

REVISION PLUS

Edexcel
GCSE Mathematics
Higher

Revision and Classroom Companion

Contents

Rounding Numbers

Rounding a Number to 1 (or more) Decimal Places

If a number is given to 1 decimal place (1 d.p.), there is one digit after the decimal point. To round a number to 1 d.p., we must look at the **second** digit after the decimal point. There are two possibilities:

1. If the second digit after the decimal point is **4 or less** (i.e. 0, 1, 2, 3 or 4) we leave the first digit after the decimal point as it is.
2. If the second digit after the decimal point is **5 or more** (i.e. 5, 6, 7, 8 or 9) we **round up** by adding 1 to the first digit after the decimal point.

To round a number to 2 d.p. we must look at the **third** digit after the decimal point to decide whether we need to round up or to keep the second digit after the decimal point the same.

To round a number to 3 d.p. we must look at the **fourth** digit and so on. Unless a question tells you otherwise, always give money to 2 decimal places. Amounts of money are rounded to 2 d.p. in exactly the same way as below.

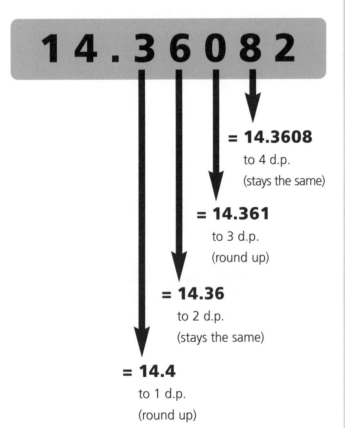

14.36082

= **14.3608**
to 4 d.p.
(stays the same)

= **14.361**
to 3 d.p.
(round up)

= **14.36**
to 2 d.p.
(stays the same)

= **14.4**
to 1 d.p.
(round up)

Rounding a Number to 1 (or more) Significant Figures

Rounding a number to a certain number of significant figures (s.f.) is very like rounding a number to a certain number of decimal places.

The number below shows the attendance at a pop concert. It has 4 significant figures.

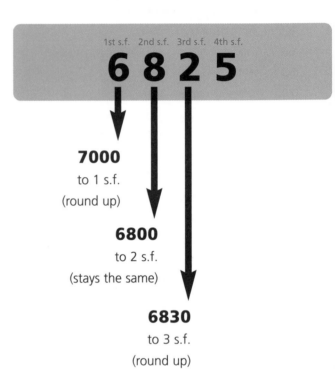

1st s.f.   2nd s.f.   3rd s.f.   4th s.f.

6 8 2 5

7000
to 1 s.f.
(round up)

6800
to 2 s.f.
(stays the same)

6830
to 3 s.f.
(round up)

Notice how 0s are used to maintain the place value of the significant figures, e.g. 6825 is 7000 to 1 s.f. not 7.

Example
To round numbers less than 1 we follow the same rules except we start counting our significant figures from the first digit greater than 0 (zero).

1st s.f.   2nd s.f.   3rd s.f.   4th s.f.

0 . 0 3 6 1 7

to 1 s.f. is **0.04** (round up)
to 2 s.f. is **0.036** (stays the same)
to 3 s.f. is **0.0362** (round up)

Ordering Decimals

Ordering decimals means rearranging a series of decimals in either ascending (lowest to highest) or descending (highest to lowest) order.

A useful method is to line up all the decimal points of the numbers in a vertical line. Then you can start with the first column on the left, and work along each column of numbers (left to right) to decide which is the biggest number.

Example
Rearrange the following in ascending order:
0.54, 5.4, 0.45, 4.5

Line up the decimal points.

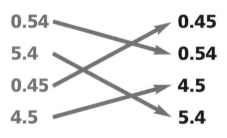

Addition and Subtraction of Decimals

When adding and subtracting decimals, you follow the same rules as for whole numbers. The place values of the digits must line up one on top of the other. An easy way is to simply line up your decimal points. Remember to bring the decimal point down to your answer.

Examples

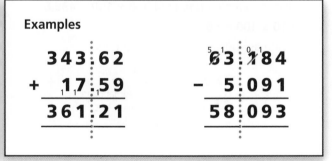

Recurring and Terminating Decimals

A **terminating decimal** is a decimal that has a finite (limited) number of decimal places.

Example
0.5 and 3.142 are terminating decimals.

A **recurring decimal** has an infinite number of decimal places in a repeating pattern.

Example
0.3333... and 0.142857142857... are recurring decimals.
- **0.3333**... may be written as **$0.\dot{3}$**
  The dot above the 3 indicates that the 3 repeats
- **0.142857142857**... may be written as **$0.\dot{1}4285\dot{7}$**
  Two dots are used here to show the start and the end of the repeating pattern

Converting Recurring Decimals into Fractions

Example
0.2727... the recurring pattern occurs after the second number

Let our recurring decimal be represented by the letter N

If the recurring pattern occurs after the first number, multiply N by 10, after the second number multiply by 100 and so on...

$$N = 0.2727...$$
$$100N = 0.2727... \times 100$$
$$100N = 27.2727...$$

Subtract N to obtain a whole number.

$$100N - N = 27.2727... - 0.2727...$$
$$99N = 27$$
$$N = \frac{27}{99} = \frac{3}{11}$$

$$0.2727... = \frac{3}{11}$$

Decimals

Multiplication of Decimal Numbers by Whole and Decimal Numbers

To multiply decimal numbers, ignore the decimal points and multiply as you would whole numbers. You put the decimal point back in at the end. In your answer, the number of digits after the decimal point should be the same as the total number of digits after the decimal points in the numbers being multiplied.

Examples

1 2.73×18

Multiply as you would whole numbers.

```
      273
   ×   18
    2730
   2,1⁵8²4
   4 9 1 4
```

Then, count the digits after the decimal point in the numbers being multiplied and transfer to answer.

$2.73 \times 18 = 49.14$

Therefore **$2.73 \times 18 = 49.14$**

2 Calculate the cost of 6.5m of carpet at £57.34 per metre. Multiply as you would whole numbers.

```
      5734
   ×    65
  34⁴40²40²
  28⁶6³17²0
  3721271210
```

$57.34 \times 6.5 = 372.710$

Insert the decimal point.

$= 372.71$

The carpet costs **£372.71**

Division of Decimal Numbers by Whole and Decimal Numbers

Division of a decimal number by a whole number is the same as the division of whole numbers. The only exception is that you must remember to take the decimal point up to your answer.

Example

$13.2 \div 6$

Divide as you would whole numbers.

```
        2.2
   6) 13.2      Remember to take
      12         the decimal point up
      ---        to the answer.
       1 2
       1 2
       ---
         0
```

Therefore **$13.2 \div 6 = 2.2$**

Division of a decimal number by another decimal number is slightly more tricky. Before you start, multiply both numbers by 10, 100, etc. until the number doing the dividing is a whole number. The process from now on is the same as the example above.

Example

$4.368 \div 0.56$

Multiply both numbers by 100 to make the divisor a whole number. **$4.368 \times 100 = 436.8$, $0.56 \times 100 = 56$**

Divide as you would whole numbers.

```
          7.8      Remember to take
   56) 436.8        the decimal point up
       392           to the answer.
       ----
        44 8
        44 8
        ----
           0
```

Therefore **$4.368 \div 0.56 = 7.8$**

Number Properties

Types of Number

Numbers can be described in many ways. Below is a summary of the types of number that you should know.

Even Numbers

Even numbers are numbers that can be divided exactly by 2. The first ten even numbers in order are…

2, 4, 6, 8, 10, 12, 14, 16, 18, 20

Odd Numbers

Since all whole numbers are either even or odd, then odd numbers are those that cannot be divided exactly by 2.

The first ten odd numbers in order are…

1, 3, 5, 7, 9, 11, 13, 15, 17, 19

Factors (Divisors)

The factors (or divisors) of a number are those whole numbers which divide exactly into it. All numbers, with the exception of square numbers (see page 9), have an even number of factors.

An easy way to find the factors of a number is to choose pairs of numbers that multiply to give that number.

Example

The factors of **10** are **1, 2, 5, 10**

(since 1 × 10 = 10, 2 × 5 = 10)

The factors of **24** are **1, 2, 3, 4, 6, 8, 12, 24**

(since 1 × 24 = 24, 2 × 12 = 24, 3 × 8 = 24, 4 × 6 = 24)

Square numbers have an odd number of factors.

Example

The factors of **16** are **1, 2, 4, 8, 16**

(since 1 × 16 = 16, 2 × 8 = 16, 4 × 4 = 16)

The factors of **36** are **1, 2, 3, 4, 6, 9, 12, 18, 36**

(since 1 × 36 = 36, 2 × 18 = 36, 3 × 12 = 36, 4 × 9 = 36, 6 × 6 = 36)

Multiples

The multiples of a number are those numbers which can be divided exactly by it. To put it simply, they are the numbers found in the 'times' tables.

The multiples of **5** are **5, 10, 15, 20, 25**, etc.

The multiples of **8** are **8, 16, 24, 32, 40**, etc.

Prime Numbers

Prime numbers are numbers that have only two factors: 1 and the number itself. The first ten prime numbers are…

2, 3, 5, 7, 11, 13, 17, 19, 23, 29

The only even prime number is 2 since all even numbers after this have 2 as a factor, which rules them out as prime numbers.

Reciprocals

The reciprocal of a number is '1 over that number'.

Examples

① The reciprocal of 4 is '1 over 4' $= \frac{1}{4}$

② The reciprocal of 0.2 is '1 over 0.2'

$$= \frac{1}{0.2} \overset{\times 10}{\underset{\times 10}{=}} \frac{10}{2} = 5$$

③ The reciprocal of $\frac{2}{3}$ is '1 over $\frac{2}{3}$'

$$= \frac{1}{\frac{2}{3}} = 1 \div \frac{2}{3} = 1 \times \frac{3}{2} = \frac{3}{2} = 1\frac{1}{2}$$

④ The reciprocal of $\frac{a}{b}$ is $\frac{b}{a}$

Any non-zero number multiplied by its reciprocal is always equal to 1.

Example

$4 \times \frac{1}{4} = \mathbf{1}$

$0.2 \times 5 = \mathbf{1}$

$\frac{2}{3} \times \frac{3}{2} = \mathbf{1}$

Number Properties

Prime Factor Form

The prime factors of a number are those prime numbers that divide exactly into it. When a number is expressed as a product of its prime factors it is said to be written in prime factor form. To find the prime factor form, try to divide your number by the lowest prime number (i.e. 2). If it works, keep repeating until it will not divide exactly. Then try the next prime number up, and continue until you have an answer of 1. This process is called **prime number decomposition**.

Examples

① Write **24** in prime factor form.

```
2 | 24
2 | 12
2 | 6
3 | 3
    1
```

so $24 = 2 \times 2 \times 2 \times 3 = 2^3 \times 3$

② Write **420** in prime factor form.

```
2 | 420
2 | 210
3 | 105
5 | 35
7 | 7
    1
```

so $420 = 2 \times 2 \times 3 \times 5 \times 7 = 2^2 \times 3 \times 5 \times 7$

Alternatively, a prime factor tree can be used to work out the prime factors of a number.

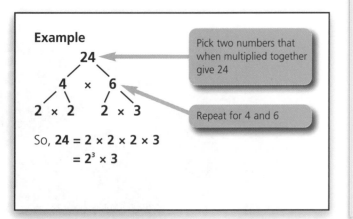

Example

Pick two numbers that when multiplied together give 24

Repeat for 4 and 6

So, $24 = 2 \times 2 \times 2 \times 3$
$= 2^3 \times 3$

Highest Common Factor

The highest common factor (HCF) of two (or more) numbers is the highest number that divides exactly into both (or all of) the numbers. To find the HCF, express your numbers in prime factor form and then select only the prime factors that are common to both numbers.

Example

What is the HCF of **24** and **90**?

First express **24** and **90** in prime factor form…

$24 = 2 \times 2 \times \boxed{2 \times 3}$
$90 = \boxed{2 \times 3} \times 3 \times 5$

… and then select prime factors that are common to both numbers.

HCF of 24 and 90 = 2 × 3 = 6

Lowest (Least) Common Multiple

The lowest (least) common multiple (LCM) of two or more numbers is the lowest number that is a multiple of all the numbers. You can use prime number decomposition to find the LCM.

Example

What is the LCM of **8** and **10**?

Write the two numbers down in prime factor form…

```
2 | 8          2 | 10
2 | 4          5 | 5
2 | 2              1
    1
```

so $8 = 2 \times 2 \times 2 = \boxed{2^3}$ so $10 = 2 \times \boxed{5}$

… and then select the highest power of each prime factor that appears and form a single multiplication.

LCM of 8 and 10 is $2^3 \times 5 = 40$

Powers

Understanding Powers

Powers or indices show that a number is to be multiplied by itself a certain number of times.

$$4 \times 4 = 4^2 \text{ (4 squared)}$$
$$4 \times 4 \times 4 = 4^3 \text{ (4 cubed)}$$
$$4 \times 4 \times 4 \times 4 = 4^4 \text{ (4 to the power 4)}$$
$$4 \times 4 \times 4 \times 4 \times 4 = 4^5 \text{ (4 to the power 5)}$$
… and so on

$$4^2$$ The power or index

Powers of Negative Numbers

Care is needed when working out powers of negative numbers.

Examples

1. $(-4)^2 = -4 \times -4 = \mathbf{16}$
   (because a 'minus' times a 'minus' is equal to a 'plus')
2. $(-4)^3 = -4 \times -4 \times -4 = \mathbf{-64}$
   (the first two 'minuses' give a 'plus'. This 'plus' times a 'minus' then gives a 'minus').

Square Numbers

Numbers obtained by squaring whole numbers are called square numbers, for example…

4 squared = 4^2 = 4 × 4 = 16
9 squared = 9^2 = 9 × 9 = 81

The first four square numbers are…

1	4	9	16
($1^2 = 1 \times 1$)	($2^2 = 2 \times 2$)	($3^2 = 3 \times 3$)	($4^2 = 4 \times 4$)

You are expected to be able to recall integer squares from 2^2 to 15^2.

$2^2=$	$3^2=$	$4^2=$	$5^2=$	$6^2=$	$7^2=$	$8^2=$
4	9	16	25	36	49	64

$9^2=$	$10^2=$	$11^2=$	$12^2=$	$13^2=$	$14^2=$	$15^2=$
81	100	121	144	169	196	225

Cube Numbers

Numbers obtained by cubing whole numbers are called cube numbers, for example…

4 cubed = 4^3 = 4 × 4 × 4 = 64
9 cubed = 9^3 = 9 × 9 × 9 = 729

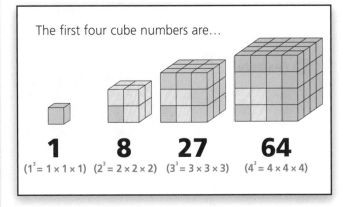

The first four cube numbers are…

1	8	27	64
($1^3 = 1 \times 1 \times 1$)	($2^3 = 2 \times 2 \times 2$)	($3^3 = 3 \times 3 \times 3$)	($4^3 = 4 \times 4 \times 4$)

This time you are expected to be able to recall the cubes of the following numbers:

$2^3=$	$3^3=$	$4^3=$	$5^3=$	$10^3=$
8	27	64	125	1000

Powers

Rules of Indices

① To multiply powers of the same number, we add the indices.
$$3^5 \times 3^2 = 3^{5+2} = 3^7, \quad 10^3 \times 10 = 10^{3+1} = 10^4$$

② To divide powers of the same number, we subtract the indices.
$$3^5 \div 3^2 = 3^{5-2} = 3^3, \quad 10^3 \div 10 = 10^{3-1} = 10^2$$

③ To raise the power of a number to another power, we multiply the indices.
$$(3^5)^2 = 3^{5\times2} = 3^{10}, \quad (10^3)^1 = 10^{3\times1} = 10^3$$

④ A number to a power of 1 is the number itself.
$$3^1 = 3$$
$$10^1 = 10$$

⑤ Any non-zero number to the power of 0 is equal to 1.
$$3^0 = 1, \quad 10^0 = 1$$
Note that 0^0 is undefined.

⑥ A number to a negative power is one over that number to the power.
$$3^{-2} = \frac{1}{3^2}$$
$$10^{-1} = \frac{1}{10^1}$$

Examples

① Evaluate $\dfrac{3^4 \times 3^7}{3^8}$

$= \dfrac{3^{4+7}}{3^8}$ — Do the multiplication first.

$= 3^{11-8}$ — Then the division.

$= 3^3$

$= 27$

② Evaluate $\dfrac{(2^4)^2}{2^{-5}}$

$= \dfrac{2^{4\times2}}{2^{-5}}$ — Do the power raised to another power first.

$= 2^{8--5}$ — Then the division. The same rules still apply for negative powers as for positive powers.

$= 2^{8+5}$

$= 2^{13}$

③ Evaluate $\dfrac{4^7 \times 4^{-2}}{4^5}$

$= \dfrac{4^{7+-2}}{4^5}$ — Do the multiplication first.

$= 4^{5-5}$ — Then the division.

$= 4^0$

$= 1$

Fractional Powers

A fractional power simply means a square root, cube root, etc. (See page 11.)

① $4^{\frac{1}{2}}$ means $\sqrt{4} = 2$...
... a power of $\frac{1}{2}$ means square root.

② $27^{\frac{1}{3}}$ means $\sqrt[3]{27} = 3$...
... a power of $\frac{1}{3}$ means cube root.

③ $10\,000^{\frac{1}{4}}$ means $\sqrt[4]{10\,000} = 10$...
... a power of $\frac{1}{4}$ means fourth root and so on.

The inverse (opposite) operation of raising a positive number to power 'n' is raising the result of this operation to power '$\frac{1}{n}$', for example...

$$4^2 = 16 \text{ and } 16^{\frac{1}{2}} = 4, \quad 5^3 = 125 \text{ and } 125^{\frac{1}{3}} = 5$$

Examples

① Calculate $8^{\frac{2}{3}}$

In this case we need to split the fractional power up into two powers, e.g. $\frac{2}{3} = \frac{1}{3} \times 2$. We can now do the calculation in two stages. Therefore...

$$8^{\frac{2}{3}} = 8^{\frac{1}{3}\times2} = 2^2 = 4$$
stage 1 stage 2

Cube root   Square
of 8 = 2   of 2 = 4

— Always do the root first (as this decreases the size of your number), and then the power.

② Calculate $32^{\frac{3}{5}}$

$$32^{\frac{3}{5}} = 32^{\frac{1}{5}\times3} = 2^3 = 8$$
stage 1 stage 2

Fifth root   Cube of
of 32 = 2   2 = 8

Roots

Square Roots of Positive Numbers

Every positive number has two square roots, for example…

$$4^2 = 16$$
$$(-4)^2 = 16$$

…therefore, 4 and -4 are both square roots of 16.

If $x^2 = 16$ then $x = \pm\sqrt{16} = \pm4$

The symbol $\sqrt{}$ is only used to represent **positive** square roots.

Since $a^2 > 0$ for any value of a, it follows that we can only find the square roots of positive numbers.

You will be expected to be able to recall the square roots of all integer squares from 2^2 **(4)** to 15^2 **(225)**.

$\sqrt{4}=$	$\sqrt{9}=$	$\sqrt{16}=$	$\sqrt{25}=$	$\sqrt{36}=$	$\sqrt{49}=$	$\sqrt{64}=$
2	3	4	5	6	7	8

$\sqrt{81}=$	$\sqrt{100}=$	$\sqrt{121}=$	$\sqrt{144}=$	$\sqrt{169}=$	$\sqrt{196}=$	$\sqrt{225}=$
9	10	11	12	13	14	15

Cube Roots of Positive Numbers

Finding the cube root of a positive number results in only one root … a positive root.

Since $4^3 = 4 \times 4 \times 4 = 64$,

then **4 is the cube root of 64**. Therefore…

$$\sqrt[3]{64} \text{ or } 64^{\frac{1}{3}} = 4$$

Similarly…

$$\sqrt[3]{125} \text{ or } 125^{\frac{1}{3}} = 5 \text{ (since } 5 \times 5 \times 5 = 125)$$

$$\sqrt[3]{1000} \text{ or } 1000^{\frac{1}{3}} = 10 \text{ (since } 10 \times 10 \times 10 = 1000)$$

Surds

Some numbers (square numbers) have an exact square root, e.g. $\sqrt{4} = 2$. Other numbers do not, e.g. $\sqrt{5} = 2.236067…$ Since $\sqrt{5}$ cannot be written as an exact number then it is more accurate to leave it as $\sqrt{5}$. When it is written in this form, $\sqrt{5}$ is called a surd. Many surds can be simplified.

Examples

1. $\sqrt{18} = \sqrt{9 \times 2} = \sqrt{9} \times \sqrt{2} = 3 \times \sqrt{2} = 3\sqrt{2}$

2. $\sqrt{48} = \sqrt{16 \times 3} = \sqrt{16} \times \sqrt{3} = 4 \times \sqrt{3} = 4\sqrt{3}$

3. $\dfrac{\sqrt{10}}{\sqrt{2}} = \sqrt{\dfrac{10}{2}} = \sqrt{5}$

   > See page 27 for multiplying out brackets.

4. $(4 - \sqrt{3})^2 = (4 - \sqrt{3})(4 - \sqrt{3})$

   $$= 16 - 4\sqrt{3} - 4\sqrt{3} + 3$$
   $$= 19 - 8\sqrt{3}$$

Decimal numbers that are neither terminating nor recurring are known as irrational numbers. All other numbers are rational. For example, the square root of 5 is 2.236067… a decimal number that does not terminate or recur. This is an example of an irrational number.

The following example shows you how to rationalise a denominator.

$$\frac{2}{\sqrt{5}} = \frac{2 \times \sqrt{5}}{\sqrt{5} \times \sqrt{5}} = \frac{2\sqrt{5}}{5}$$

> Multiply the numerator (top number) and denominator (bottom number) by the denominator itself, e.g. $\sqrt{5}$.

The denominator is now a rational number.

Sometimes we need to make use of the algebraic result $(a + b)(a - b) = a^2 - b^2$ to rationalise a denominator.

Example

$$\frac{8}{3 - \sqrt{5}} = \frac{8}{3 - \sqrt{5}} \times \frac{3 + \sqrt{5}}{3 + \sqrt{5}}$$

$$= \frac{8(3 + \sqrt{5})}{3^2 - 5}$$

$$= \frac{8(3 + \sqrt{5})}{4}$$

$$= 2(3 + \sqrt{5})$$

Order of Operations

Bidmas

The simplest possible calculation involves only one operation, e.g. an addition or multiplication.

However, when a calculation involves more than one operation, you must carry them out in the order shown here.

BIDMAS

| Brackets | Indices (or powers) | Divisions and Multiplications – these can be done in any order | Additions and Subtractions – these can be done in any order |

Examples

1 $8 + 3 \times 4$

Do the multiplication first

$= 8 + 12$

Then the addition

$= 20$

2 $\dfrac{(14 + 6)}{-4}$

Do the addition in the bracket first

$= \dfrac{20}{-4}$ ($+ \div - = -$)

Then the division

$= -5$

3 $4^2 - 2 \times 5$

Work out the square first

$= 16 - 2 \times 5$

Then the multiplication

$= 16 - 10$

Then the subtraction

$= 6$

4 4×3^2 ← A common mistake is to work out $4 \times 3 = 12^2 = 144$.

Work out the square first

$= 4 \times 9$

Then the multiplication

$= 36$

Use of Brackets

Inserting brackets into a calculation changes the order in which the operations are carried out and this produces different answers.

Examples

1 Here is a calculation without brackets.

$8 + 3 \times 4 - 2 = 8 + 12 - 2 = 20 - 2 = 18$
(or 8 + 10)

If we now insert one pair of brackets into the calculation we can obtain...

$(8 + 3) \times 4 - 2 = 11 \times 4 - 2 = 44 - 2 = 42$
$8 + 3 \times (4 - 2) = 8 + 3 \times 2 = 8 + 6 = 14$

2 The diagram represents part of a garden that is to be paved. The cost of the paving is £15 per m². Calculate the total cost.

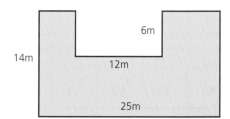

The total cost in £ is given by
$(25 \times 14 - 12 \times 6) \times 15$

= **£4170**

Enter this on a calculator as it looks written here

Standard Index Form

What is Standard Index Form?

Standard index form is a way of writing numbers that makes it easier to deal with very large and very small numbers.

A number written as $a \times 10^n$, where $1 \leqslant a < 10$ and n is an integer, is written in standard index form.

For **large** numbers, n is a **positive integer** and is equal to the number of places the decimal point has moved.

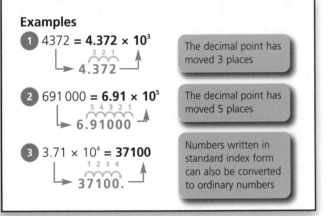

Examples

1. $4372 = \textbf{4.372} \times \textbf{10}^3$

   The decimal point has moved 3 places

2. $691\,000 = \textbf{6.91} \times \textbf{10}^5$

   The decimal point has moved 5 places

3. $3.71 \times 10^4 = \textbf{37100}$

   Numbers written in standard index form can also be converted to ordinary numbers

For **small** positive numbers, n is a **negative integer** (**min**us for **min**ute numbers) and is equal to the number of places the decimal point has moved.

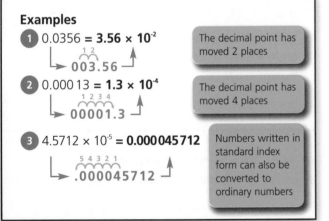

Examples

1. $0.0356 = \textbf{3.56} \times \textbf{10}^{-2}$

   The decimal point has moved 2 places

2. $0.000\,13 = \textbf{1.3} \times \textbf{10}^{-4}$

   The decimal point has moved 4 places

3. $4.5712 \times 10^{-5} = \textbf{0.000\,045\,712}$

   Numbers written in standard index form can also be converted to ordinary numbers

Calculations with Standard Index Form

To add or subtract numbers written in standard index form, convert to 'ordinary numbers', do the calculation and then, if required, change your answer back into standard index form.

To multiply or divide numbers written in standard index form, carry out separate calculations for the numbers and powers and then rearrange your answer back into standard index form.

Examples

1. $4.2 \times 10^4 + 8.6 \times 10^3$

   $= 42000 + 8600$

   $= 50600$

   $= \textbf{5.06} \times \textbf{10}^4$

2. $9.37 \times 10^{-2} - 1.6 \times 10^{-3}$

   $= 0.0937 - 0.0016$

   $= 0.0921$

   $= \textbf{9.21} \times \textbf{10}^{-2}$

3. $3.2 \times 10^{-3} \times 4.5 \times 10^{-4}$

   $= (3.2 \times 4.5) \times (10^{-3} \times 10^{-4})$

   $= 14.4 \times 10^{-7}$

   $= \textbf{1.44} \times \textbf{10}^1 \times \textbf{10}^{-7} = \textbf{1.44} \times \textbf{10}^{-6}$

4. $5.6 \times 10^5 \div 8 \times 10^1$

   $= (5.6 \div 8) \times (10^5 \div 10^1)$

   $= 0.7 \times 10^4$

   $= \textbf{7} \times \textbf{10}^{-1} \times \textbf{10}^4 = \textbf{7} \times \textbf{10}^3$

5. Light travels at 186000 miles per second. A light year is the distance that light will travel in one year. The number of miles in a light year is given by…

   $186\,000 \times 60 \times 60 \times 24 \times 365$

   Complete this calculation and give your answer in standard form.

   $= \textbf{5.87} \times \textbf{10}^{12}$ The answer is too large to be displayed as an ordinary number on a calculator. It is automatically given in standard form.

Ordering Numbers in Standard Index Form

To order numbers in standard index form, first look at the value of n. The largest numbers have the highest powers of 10. For numbers with the same value of n, compare the values of a.

Example

Write these numbers in descending order
7.8×10^5, 3.2×10^8, 6.5×10^5.
The number with the largest value of n is 3.2×10^8.
The other two numbers have the same value of n but $7.8 > 6.5$ so in descending order the numbers are…
$\textbf{3.2} \times \textbf{10}^8, \textbf{7.8} \times \textbf{10}^5, \textbf{6.5} \times \textbf{10}^5$

Fractions

Understanding Simple Fractions

The diagram shows a whole pizza that has been cut into four equal parts (or slices). Each slice can be described as a fraction of the whole pizza and its value is $\frac{1}{4}$.

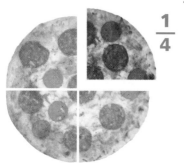

$$\frac{1}{4}$$

The pizza however could have been cut into any number of slices, where each slice is a different fraction of the whole pizza (see the diagrams below).

The top number of a fraction is called the **numerator**, while the bottom number is called the **denominator**.

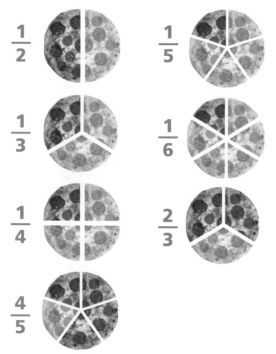

$\frac{1}{2}$ $\frac{1}{5}$

$\frac{1}{3}$ $\frac{1}{6}$

$\frac{1}{4}$ $\frac{2}{3}$

$\frac{4}{5}$

Equivalent Fractions

Equivalent Fractions are fractions that are equal. You can build chains of equivalent fractions by multiplying the numerator and denominator in the fraction by the same number.

$$\overset{\times 2}{\frac{1}{4}} = \overset{\times 3}{\frac{2}{8}} = \overset{\times 4}{\frac{6}{24}} = \frac{24}{96}$$
$$\underset{\times 2}{\quad} \underset{\times 3}{\quad} \underset{\times 4}{\quad}$$

Cancelling Fractions

You can also divide the numerator and denominator in a fraction by the same number. Chains of equivalent fractions that are cancelled down using division always come to an end when the fraction is expressed in its simplest form, i.e. lowest terms.

$$\overset{\div 3}{\frac{18}{27}} = \overset{\div 3}{\frac{6}{9}} = \frac{2}{3} \text{ or } \overset{\div 9}{\frac{18}{27}} = \frac{2}{3}$$
$$\underset{\div 3}{\quad} \underset{\div 3}{\quad} \underset{\div 9}{\quad}$$

Ordering Fractions

To put fractions in order, first we need to write each fraction with a common denominator.

> **Example**
> Arrange $\frac{9}{10}, \frac{4}{5}, \frac{7}{8}$ in ascending order.
>
> The lowest common multiple of 10, 5 and 8 is 40.
>
> $$\overset{\times 4}{\frac{9}{10}} = \frac{36}{40} \quad \overset{\times 8}{\frac{4}{5}} = \frac{32}{40} \quad \overset{\times 5}{\frac{7}{8}} = \frac{35}{40}$$
> $$\underset{\times 4}{\quad} \underset{\times 8}{\quad} \underset{\times 5}{\quad}$$
>
> If we now compare the numerators we can arrange the fractions in ascending (lowest to highest) order.
>
> In ascending order they are: $\frac{4}{5}, \frac{7}{8}, \frac{9}{10}$.

When you have fractions with common denominators, it is possible to find other fractions that lie between them.

For example, as seen above $\frac{4}{5} = \frac{32}{40}$ and $\frac{7}{8} = \frac{35}{40}$.

We can write two other fractions with denominator 40, which are greater than $\frac{4}{5}$ but less than $\frac{7}{8}$. They would be $\frac{33}{40}$ and $\frac{34}{40}$, which cancels down to $\frac{17}{20}$.

Calculations with Fractions

Addition of Fractions

Two fractions can be added very easily providing they have a common denominator.

Example

$\frac{2}{5} = \frac{8}{20}$ $\frac{2}{5} + \frac{3}{4}$ $\frac{3}{4} = \frac{15}{20}$

$= \frac{8}{20} + \frac{15}{20}$

$= \frac{23}{20}$

$= \mathbf{1\frac{3}{20}}$

With mixed numbers, add the whole numbers and fractions separately and then combine.

Example

$2\frac{2}{3} + 3\frac{1}{7}$

$= (2 + 3) + (\frac{2}{3} + \frac{1}{7})$

$= 5 + (\frac{14}{21} + \frac{3}{21})$

$= \mathbf{5\frac{17}{21}}$

Subtraction of Fractions

As with addition, two fractions can be subtracted very easily providing they have common denominators.

Example

$\frac{7}{8} = \frac{21}{24}$ $\frac{7}{8} - \frac{2}{3}$ $\frac{2}{3} = \frac{16}{24}$

$= \frac{21}{24} - \frac{16}{24}$

$= \mathbf{\frac{5}{24}}$

With mixed numbers, subtract the whole numbers and fractions separately and then combine.

Example

$4\frac{1}{2} - 1\frac{4}{5}$

$= (4 - 1) + (\frac{1}{2} - \frac{4}{5})$

$= 3 + (\frac{5}{10} - \frac{8}{10})$

$= 3 + (-\frac{3}{10})$

$= 3 - \frac{3}{10} = \mathbf{2\frac{7}{10}}$

Alternatively, you can use improper fractions.

$4\frac{1}{2} - 1\frac{4}{5}$

$= \frac{9}{2} - \frac{9}{5}$

$= \frac{45}{10} - \frac{18}{10}$

$= \frac{27}{10}$

$= 2\frac{7}{10}$

Multiplication and Division of Fractions

To multiply two fractions, multiply the two numerators together and multiply the two denominators together.

Example

$\frac{2}{3} \times \frac{4}{5} = \frac{2\times4}{3\times5} = \mathbf{\frac{8}{15}}$

Division of two fractions is the same as multiplication, except that you turn the second fraction (that is doing the dividing) upside down and change the division sign to a multiplication sign.

Example

$\frac{2}{3} \div \frac{4}{5} = \frac{2}{3} \times \frac{5}{4} = \frac{2\times5}{3\times4} = \frac{10}{12} = \mathbf{\frac{5}{6}}$

To divide by a fraction, multiply by its reciprocal

To multiply or divide mixed numbers you have to convert them to improper fractions first.

Examples

1 $2\frac{1}{2} \times 1\frac{1}{6} = \frac{5}{2} \times \frac{7}{6}$

$= \frac{5\times7}{2\times6}$

$= \frac{35}{12}$

$= \mathbf{2\frac{11}{12}}$

2 $1\frac{1}{3} \div 3\frac{1}{2} = \frac{4}{3} \div \frac{7}{2}$

$= \frac{4}{3} \times \frac{2}{7}$

$= \frac{4\times2}{3\times7}$

$= \mathbf{\frac{8}{21}}$

To multiply or divide a fraction by an integer, convert the integer to an improper fraction. For example, 4 as an improper fraction is $\frac{4}{1}$. You can then do the multiplication or division as normal.

Examples

1 $\frac{4}{7} \times 3 = \frac{4}{7} \times \frac{3}{1}$

$= \frac{4\times3}{7\times1}$

$= \frac{12}{7}$

$= \mathbf{1\frac{5}{7}}$

2 $\frac{2}{3} \div 10 = \frac{2}{3} \div \frac{10}{1}$

$= \frac{2}{3} \times \frac{1}{10}$

$= \frac{2\times1}{3\times10}$

$= \frac{2}{30}$

$= \mathbf{\frac{1}{15}}$

Calculations with Fractions

Calculating a Fraction of a Quantity

To find a fraction of any quantity, you have to multiply the fraction by the quantity. In other words, 'of' means 'times' or 'multiply' (×).

Examples

① Calculate $\frac{4}{5}$ of 60kg.

$$\frac{4}{5} \text{ of } 60\text{kg} = \frac{4}{5} \times 60 \quad \boxed{\text{'of' means '×'}}$$

$$= \frac{4}{5} \times \frac{60}{1} = \frac{240}{5} = \textbf{48kg}$$

Alternatively: $\frac{4}{\cancel{5}_1} \times \frac{\cancel{60}^{12}}{1} = \frac{48}{1} = \textbf{48kg}$

② A brand new car costing £9000 will lose $\frac{1}{5}$ of its value in the first year. What is the value of the car after the first year?

Before we can calculate its value we need to calculate the loss.

$$\text{Loss} = \frac{1}{5} \text{ of } £9000 = \frac{1}{5} \times 9000$$

$$\boxed{\text{'of' means '×'}}$$

$$= \frac{9000}{5} = £1800$$

Value of car after the first year

$$= £9000 - £1800 = \textbf{£7200}$$

$$\boxed{\begin{array}{l} \text{OR } 1 - \frac{1}{5} = \frac{4}{5} \text{ of value after first year} \\ = £9000 \times \frac{4}{5} = \frac{36\,000}{5} = \textbf{£7200} \end{array}}$$

③ A marathon runner covers a distance of $12\frac{1}{2}$ miles in $1\frac{1}{4}$ hours on a training run. What is his average speed?

$$\boxed{\textbf{Average speed} = \frac{\textbf{Distance}}{\textbf{Time}}}$$

$$= 12\frac{1}{2} \div 1\frac{1}{4}$$

$$= \frac{25}{2} \div \frac{5}{4}$$

$$= \frac{\cancel{25}^5}{\cancel{2}_1} \times \frac{\cancel{4}^2}{\cancel{5}_1}$$

$$= \frac{10}{1}$$

$$= \textbf{10 miles per hour}$$

Expressing One Quantity as a Fraction of Another Quantity

To express one quantity as a fraction of another, firstly, you must make sure that both quantities are in the same units. Then, to express the relationship as a fraction, the first quantity becomes the numerator (top number) and the second quantity becomes the denominator (bottom number). If need be, write the fraction in its lowest terms.

Examples

① Write 30 out of 120 as a fraction.

$$30 \text{ out of } 120 = \frac{30}{120} = \frac{1}{4}$$

② Express 36 seconds as a fraction of 2 minutes.

Both quantities must be in the same units, so change 2 minutes into seconds.
2 minutes = 2 × 60s = 120s, so...

$$36\text{s as a fraction of } 120\text{s} = \frac{36}{120} = \frac{3}{10}$$

Percentages

Understanding Simple Percentages

Percentages are used in everyday life, from pay rises to price reductions. They help us to make easy comparisons. When you understand the basics of percentages they are even easier than decimals or fractions.

Percentages focus on the whole being equal to one hundred, i.e. the whole is one hundred percent. So, if someone gives you 50% of a whole pizza this tells you the 'number of parts per 100' you have, e.g. 50% is 50 parts per 100 or $\frac{50}{100}$.

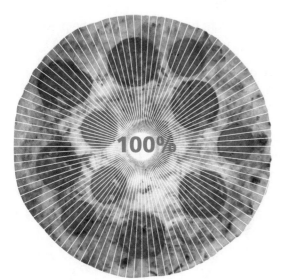

100%

10%

40%
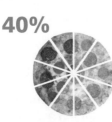

20%

50%

30%

etc.

Calculating a Percentage of a Quantity

Examples

1 Calculate 40% of 50cm.

> 40% means 40 parts per 100 or $\frac{40}{100}$ and 'of' means 'times' or 'multiply'(×).

$$40\% \text{ of } 50cm = \frac{40}{100} \times 50 = \frac{40 \times 50}{100} = \frac{2000}{100}$$
$$= 20cm$$

2 Calculate 15% of £4.80. Give your answer in pence.

£4.80 = 4.80 × 100p = 480p

> 15% means 15 parts out of 100 or $\frac{15}{100}$ and 'of' means 'times' (×).

$$15\% \text{ of } 480p = \frac{15}{100} \times 480$$
$$= \frac{\overset{3}{15} \times \overset{24}{480}}{\underset{\underset{1}{20}}{100}}$$
$$= \frac{72}{1}$$
$$= 72p$$

Expressing One Quantity as a Percentage of Another Quantity

Make sure that both quantities are in the same units. Firstly, express one quantity as a fraction of the other, where the first quantity becomes the numerator (top number) and the second quantity becomes the denominator (bottom number). Then multiply the fraction by 100%.

Examples

1 Write 18 out of 30 as a percentage.

$$18 \text{ out of } 30 = \frac{18}{30} \times 100\%$$
$$= \frac{\overset{3}{18} \times \overset{20}{100}}{\underset{5}{30}_{1}} = 60\%$$

2 Express 30cm as a percentage of 3m. Both quantities must be in the same units, so change 3m into centimetres.
3m = 3 × 100cm = 300cm, so...

$$30cm \text{ as a } \% \text{ of } 300cm = \frac{30}{300} \times 100\%$$
$$= \frac{\overset{1}{30} \times 100}{\underset{10}{300}} = 10\%$$

Percentage Change

Calculations Involving Comparisons

These are calculations where the original amount has been increased or decreased by a certain percentage. You must remember that the original amount is always equal to 100% and that the transformed amount will always be a percentage that is above or below 100%.

Examples

1 A standard box of breakfast cereal weighs 500g. Special boxes contain an extra 25%. Calculate the weight of a special box of cereal.

Firstly calculate the increase in weight...

$25\% \text{ of } 500g = \dfrac{25}{100} \times 500g$

$= \dfrac{\overset{1}{\cancel{25}} \times \overset{125}{\cancel{500}}}{\underset{\underset{1}{\cancel{4}}}{\cancel{100}}}$

$= \textbf{125g}$

... then add it to the weight of a standard box of cereal.

Weight of special box = 500g + 125g = **625g**

> An alternative method would be as follows: A standard box of cereal is to be increased by 25%. If a standard box is 100%, a special box will be 100% + 25% = 125%.
>
> $125\% = \dfrac{125}{100} = \textbf{1.25}$
>
> In other words, the weight of a special box is 1.25 times the weight of a standard box.
>
> **500 × 1.25 = 625g**

2 On 1st January John's weight is 80kg. In the first six months of the year his weight increases by 10%, followed by a 10% decrease in the second six months of the year. What is his weight at the end of the year?

After the first six months, his weight is 100% + 10% = 110% of his original weight.

$110\% = \dfrac{110}{100} = \textbf{1.1}$

i.e. his weight is now 1.1 times its original amount.

After the second six months, his weight is 100% − 10% = 90% of his weight at the end of the first six months.

$90\% = \dfrac{90}{100} = \textbf{0.9}$

i.e. his weight becomes 0.9 times the previous amount, which is actually a decrease.

Weight at the end of the year =
80 × 1.1 × 0.9 = **79.2kg**

3 A bouncing ball is dropped from a height of 5m. It reaches 80% of its previous height after every bounce. How high does it reach after the third bounce?

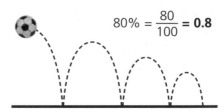

$80\% = \dfrac{80}{100} = \textbf{0.8}$

So, the height the ball reaches is 0.8 times the previous height reached.

After 3 bounces, height reached
= 5m × 0.8 × 0.8 × 0.8 = **2.56m**

> This is an example of a repeated multiplier:
> $0.8 \times 0.8 \times 0.8 = 0.8^3$ (0.8 to the power 3).
> So, you could simply write...
>
> **After 3 bounces, height reached**
> = 5m × 0.8^3 = 5m × 0.512 = **2.56m**

Percentage Change

Examples

4 A shop offers 10% off all its clothes. A shirt has a sale price of £27. What was the original price of the shirt?

Original price of shirt = 100%
Sale price of shirt   = 100% − 10%
**   = 90%**

> There has been a decrease of 10%

∴ ÷90 ×100

90% = £27
1% = £0.30
100% = £30

÷90 ×100

So the original price of the shirt was £30

> Alternatively you could calculate...
>
> ×0.9
>
> **Original price   Sale price**
>
> ÷0.9
>
> **Original price of shirt = £27 ÷ 0.9**
> **   = £30**

5 A company allocates £15 000 of its budget to be spent on advertising. This is a 20% increase on the money budgeted for advertising last year. How much money did the company budget for advertising last year?

The original amount in this question is the money budgeted for advertising last year.

Advertising budget last year = 100%
Advertising budget this year = 100% + 20%

> There has been an increase of 20%

= 120%

÷120 ∴ ×100

120% = £15 000
1% = £125
100% = £12 500

÷120 ×100

So the advertising budget last year was £12 500

> Alternatively you could calculate...
>
> ×1.2
>
> **Last year's budget   this year's budget**
>
> ÷1.2
>
> **Last year's budget = £15 000 ÷ 1.2 = £12 500**

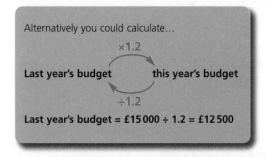

Ratios

What is a Ratio?

A ratio is a comparison between two or more quantities. The image shows two columns of coins. The first column has ten £1 coins and the second column has six 2p coins. To compare the two sets of coins we can say that the ratio of the number of £1 coins to 2p coins is…

10 to 6 or 10 : 6

Ratios can be simplified into their simplest form, just like fractions…

$$÷2 \overset{\textbf{10 : 6}}{\underset{\textbf{= 5 : 3}}{\frown}} ÷2$$

A ratio of **5 : 3** means that for every five £1 coins there are three 2p coins.

The above ratio can be written in the form **1 : n** by dividing both numbers in the ratio by 5…

$$÷5 \overset{\textbf{5 : 3}}{\underset{\textbf{= 1 : 0.6}}{\frown}} ÷5$$

It could also be written in the form **n : 1** by dividing both numbers in the ratio by 3…

$$÷3 \overset{\textbf{5 : 3}}{\underset{\textbf{= 1.\dot{6} : 1}}{\frown}} ÷3$$

Examples

1 A bag of carrots weighs 300g and a bag of potatoes 1.5kg. Calculate the ratio of weight of carrots to weight of potatoes.

Both quantities must be in the same units so, 1.5kg = 1.5 × 1000g = **1500g**

Ratio of weight of carrots to weight of potatoes is…

$$÷300 \overset{\textbf{300g : 1500g}}{\underset{\textbf{= 1 : 5}}{\frown}} ÷300$$

2 On a map, a distance of 6km is shown as 3cm. Write the map distance to the real distance as a ratio in its simplest form.

The ratio is 3cm : 6km
= 3cm : 6 × 1000 × 100cm
= 3 : 600 000
= **1 : 200 000**

> Make the units the same for both parts of the ratio, then simplify by cancelling the units and any common factors.

Ratios and Fractions

A ratio can be written as a fraction and vice versa.

Examples

1 If $\frac{2}{5}$ of a class are boys what is the ratio of boys to girls? Give your answer in the form 1 : n

The ratio of boys to girls is therefore…

$$×5 \overset{\frac{2}{5} : \frac{3}{5}}{\underset{\textbf{= 2 : 3}}{\frown}} ×5$$

Written in the form **1 : n** it is…

$$×5 \overset{\textbf{2 : 3}}{\underset{\textbf{= 1 : 1.5}}{\frown}} ×5$$

In other words for any one boy in the class there are one and a half girls.

2 A drink is made by mixing cordial and water in the ratio 1 : 4. What fraction of the drink is cordial?

1 part out of 5 (1 + 4) parts is cordial.
The fraction of the drink that is cordial is $\frac{1}{5}$.

3 John mixes concrete by using cement, sand and gravel in the ratio 1 : 2 : 3. What fraction of the mix is sand?

2 parts out of 6 (1 + 2 + 3) parts is sand.
The fraction of the cement that is sand is $\frac{2}{6} = \frac{1}{3}$

Calculations with Ratios

Dividing a Quantity in a Given Ratio

Examples

1. £60 is to be divided between Jon and Pat in the ratio 2 : 3. How much money does each one receive?

   We need to divide £60 in the ratio 2 : 3.

   The digits in the ratio represent parts. Jon gets 2 parts and Pat gets 3 parts. The total number of parts is 2 + 3 = 5 parts, which is equal to £60. Therefore…

   $$\div 5 \left(\begin{array}{c} \textbf{5 parts = £60} \\ \textbf{1 part = £12} \end{array} \right) \div 5$$

   Since we now know the 'value' of 1 part we can work out how much money Jon and Pat get.

   Jon gets 2 parts = 2 × £12 = £24
   Pat gets 3 parts = 3 × £12 = £36

   > Check: £24 + £36 = £60

2. Three brothers aged 6, 9 and 15 decide to share a tin of toffees in the ratio of their ages. If the tin contains 240 toffees how many toffees does each brother get?

   We need to divide 240 toffees in the ratio 6 : 9 : 15

   > Whenever possible cancel down your ratio to make things simpler

   $$\div 3 \left(\begin{array}{c} \textbf{6 : 9 : 15} \\ \textbf{= 2 : 3 : 5} \end{array} \right) \div 3$$

   Total number of parts
   = 2 + 3 + 5 = 10 parts

   Therefore…

   $$\div 10 \left(\begin{array}{c} \textbf{10 parts = 240 toffees} \\ \textbf{1 part = 24 toffees} \end{array} \right) \div 10$$

   Brother aged 6 gets 2 × 24 = 48 toffees
   Brother aged 9 gets 3 × 24 = 72 toffees
   Brother aged 15 gets 5 × 24 = 120 toffees

   > Check: 48 + 72 + 120 = 240 toffees

Increasing and Decreasing a Quantity in Direct Proportion

Examples

A recipe to make 10 flapjacks requires, among other ingredients, 180g of butter. How much butter does a cook need to use if they want to make…
a) 6 flapjacks?
b) 25 flapjacks?

This is an example of a quantity (e.g. butter) that increases or decreases in direct proportion to the amount of baking needed. The more baking needed the greater the amount of butter needed and vice versa.

The easiest way is to work out the amount of butter needed to make 1 flapjack.

$$\div 10 \left(\begin{array}{c} \textbf{10 flapjacks require 180g of butter} \\ \textbf{1 flapjack requires 18g of butter} \end{array} \right) \div 10$$

a) **6 flapjacks require**
    6 × 18g = 108g of butter

b) **25 flapjacks require**
    25 × 18g = 450g of butter

Direct and Inverse Proportion

Direct Proportion

Two quantities are in **direct proportion** if, for example, when we double (or treble) one quantity the other quantity also doubles (or trebles).

Let us take two quantities, y and x, that are directly proportional. We can say that…

y is directly proportional to x or $y \propto x$,

which means that…

$y = kx$ where k is a constant,

i.e. k is a number that doesn't change.

Whenever you answer questions involving two quantities that are in direct proportion, the first thing to do is find the value of k to give you the formula for the relationship between the two quantities.

Example

The distance, d, travelled by a cyclist is directly proportional to t, the time of travel. If the cyclist travels 40 metres in 5 seconds, how far will the same cyclist travel in 12 seconds?

We know that $d \propto t$ or $d = kt$. The first thing we do is find the value for k.

Since $d = \textbf{40m}$ when $t = \textbf{5s}$ this gives us…

$40 = k \times 5$

$\therefore k = \dfrac{40}{5} = 8$

Our relationship now becomes…

$d = kt = 8 \times t$

$\quad = 8t$

We can now work out the value of d when $t = 12$s

$d = 8t = 8 \times 12$

$\quad = \textbf{96m}$

Inverse Proportion

Two quantities are in **inverse proportion** if, for example, when we double (or treble) one of the quantities the other quantity halves (or is divided by 3).

Let us take two quantities, y and x, that are inversely proportional. We can say that…

y is inversely proportional to x or $y \propto \dfrac{1}{x}$,

which means that…

$y = \dfrac{k}{x}$ where k is a constant

Whenever you answer questions involving two quantities that are inversely proportional, the first thing to do is find the value of k to give the formula for the relationship between the two quantities.

Example

The current, I, passing through an electrical component is inversely proportional to the resistance, R, of the component. If the current is 0.4 amps when the resistance is 20 ohms, calculate the current when the resistance is 50 ohms.

We know that $I \propto \dfrac{1}{R}$ or $I = \dfrac{k}{R}$. Again, the first thing we do is find the value of k.

Since $I = \textbf{0.4 amps}$ when $R = \textbf{20 ohms}$, this gives us…

$0.4 = \dfrac{k}{20}$

$\therefore k = \textbf{0.4} \times \textbf{20} = \textbf{8}$

Our relationship now becomes…

$I = \dfrac{k}{R} = \dfrac{8}{R}$

So, we can now work out I when $R = \textbf{50 ohms}$.

$I = \dfrac{8}{R} = \dfrac{8}{50}$

$\quad = \textbf{0.16 amps}$

What are Upper and Lower Bounds?

Sometimes measurements are given to a certain degree of accuracy. When this happens the actual measurement (or quantity) lies within a range that has its limits a certain value below (the **lower bound**) to a certain value above (the **upper bound**) the given measurement.

Accuracy of Given Measurement	Limits of Range Measurement Lies Between
Nearest 1000	500 below to 500 above the given measurement
Nearest 100	50 below to 50 above the given measurement
Nearest 10	5 below to 5 above the given measurement
Nearest 1	0.5 below to 0.5 above the given measurement
Nearest 0.1	0.05 below to 0.05 above the given measurement

Upper and Lower Bounds for the Four Rules of Number

If **A = 50** to the nearest **10 (45 ≤ A < 55)** and **B = 30** to the nearest **10 (25 ≤ B < 35)** then…

> The actual value cannot be equal to the upper bound because if it was, when rounded to the nearest 10, A = 60 and B = 40.

	Upper Bound	Lower Bound
A + B	55 + 35 = 90	45 + 25 = 70
A − B	55 − 25 = 30	45 − 35 = 10
A × B	55 × 35 = 1925	45 × 25 = 1125
A ÷ B	55 ÷ 25 = 2.2	45 ÷ 35 = 1.29 (2 d.p.)

Examples

1 A sprinter runs 200m in a time of 20.2 seconds, which is measured to the nearest 0.1 of a second. What are the upper and lower bounds of the time taken?

A measurement to the nearest 0.1s means that the actual measurement lies somewhere in a range 0.05s above or below the time of 20.2s. In other words there is a possible error of ± 0.05s on the recorded time.

Lower bound = 20.2s − 0.05s = 20.15s
Upper bound = 20.2s + 0.05s = 20.25s

This can be written: **20.15s ≤ t < 20.25s** where t = **time taken**

> The actual value cannot be equal to the upper bound because if it was, the time to the nearest 0.1s would be 20.3s.

2 The rectangle below has dimensions 3cm by 2cm; each length is correct to the nearest centimetre. What is the smallest and largest area possible for the rectangle?

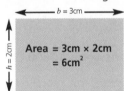

Area = 3cm × 2cm = 6cm²

> The measurement of the base, **b**, can be anywhere in the range **2.5cm ≤ b < 3.5cm**

> The measurement of the height, **h**, can be anywhere in the range **1.5cm ≤ h < 2.5cm**

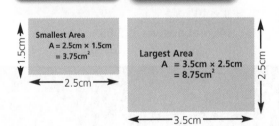

Smallest Area
A = 2.5cm × 1.5cm = 3.75cm²

Largest Area
A = 3.5cm × 2.5cm = 8.75cm²

Smallest Area = 3.75cm²
Largest Area = 8.75cm²

Strictly speaking, this is not the largest value of the area, **Acm²**, as **3.75cm² ≤ A < 8.75cm²**. In practice, however, the upper bound is used as the largest area.

Estimating and Checking

Estimating Answers

Answers to many calculations can be estimated by rounding off numbers within the calculations to 1 significant figure.

> **Examples**
> Estimate the answers to the following calculations:
>
> **1**   71 + 18 − 26
> $\approx$ 70 + 20 − 30
> $\approx$ **60 (Actual answer is 63)**
>
> **2** $\dfrac{3.6 \times 10.4}{7.7 - 3.1}$
>
> $\approx \dfrac{4 \times 10}{8 - 3}$
>
> $\approx \dfrac{40}{5}$
>
> $\approx$ **8 (Actual answer is 8.14 (2 d.p.))**
>
> **3** $\dfrac{413 \times 4.87}{0.189}$
>
> $\approx \dfrac{400 \times 5}{0.2}$
>
> $\approx \dfrac{2000}{0.2}$
>
> $\approx$ **10 000**
> **(Actual answer is 10 600 (3 s.f.))**
>
> **4** $\dfrac{57341}{0.00216}$
>
> $= \dfrac{5.7341 \times 10^4}{2.16 \times 10^{-3}}$
>
> See page 13 for Standard Form
>
> $\approx \dfrac{6 \times 10^4}{2 \times 10^{-3}}$
>
> $\approx$ **3 × 10⁷** $\;(\approx 3 \times 10^7)$
> **(Actual answer is 2.65 × 10⁷)**

Checking your Answers for Accuracy

Answers to calculations can be checked for accuracy by starting with your answer and working backwards, reversing the operations.

> **Examples**
> **1**   8 × 7 = 56 $\longrightarrow$ $\dfrac{56}{8} = 7$ ✓ or $\dfrac{56}{7} = 8$ ✓
>
> **2**   The table below shows the amount of money collected by a small local charity from October to December, using collecting tins at three different locations. Check it for accuracy.

Month	Location 1	Location 2	Location 3	Total
Oct	28.08	16.73	18.23	63.04
Nov	32.96	21.01	18.16	72.13
Dec	26.12	19.57	16.03	61.72
Total	87.16	57.31	52.42	**196.89**

For this example, there are several ways of checking it for accuracy. You could check the totals for each month (rows) or the totals for each location (columns). Finally, check the overall total.

- 63.04 + 72.13 + 61.72 = **196.89**
  196.89 − 61.72 − 72.13 = **63.04** ✓

- 87.16 + 57.31 + 52.42 = **196.89**
  196.89 − 52.42 − 57.31 = **87.16** ✓

STRAY CAT FUND

Expressions and Identities

xy

Algebra is a branch of mathematics where letters and other symbols are used to represent numbers and quantities in expressions, equations, identities and formulae. Algebra follows the same rules as arithmetic.

Algebraic Expressions

An algebraic expression is a collection of connected letters, numbers and arithmetical symbols. Here are some simple expressions and their meanings.

Algebraic Expression	What it Means
$2a$	$a + a$ or $2 \times a$
ab	$a \times b$ (or $b \times a$)
$\dfrac{a}{b}$	$a \div b$
$3a - b$	$(3 \times a) - b$
c^2	$c \times c$
$4mn$	$4 \times m \times n$
x^2	$x \times x$
a^3	$a \times a \times a$
$4x^2y$	$4 \times x \times x \times y$
$(4a)^2$	$4a \times 4a$

Collecting Like Terms

Many expressions can be simplified by collecting together like terms, e.g. all the x's or all the x^2's.

Examples

1. $a + 2a$ is **$3a$**

2. $5x - 8x + 7x$ is **$4x$**

> When your expression contains 'different' terms, rearrange and collect together all like terms before you simplify.

3. $6b + 3c - 4b$
   $= \underbrace{6b - 4b}_{\text{Like terms}} + 3c$
   $= \mathbf{2b + 3c}$

4. $4x + 7y - x - 3y$
   $= \underbrace{4x - x}_{\text{Like terms}} + \underbrace{7y - 3y}_{\text{Like terms}}$
   $= \mathbf{3x + 4y}$

5. $8x^2 - 4x + 3 - 3x^2 + 7x - 8$
   $= \underbrace{8x^2 - 3x^2}_{\text{Like terms}} \underbrace{- 4x + 7x}_{\text{Like terms}} + \underbrace{3 - 8}_{\text{Like terms}}$
   $= \mathbf{5x^2 + 3x - 5}$

6. $5pq - 7rs + 8qp + 2sr$
   $= \underbrace{5pq + 8pq}_{\substack{\text{Like terms} \\ \text{since '}pq\text{'} \\ \text{is the same} \\ \text{as '}qp\text{'}}} \underbrace{- 7rs + 2rs}_{\substack{\text{Like terms} \\ \text{since '}rs\text{' is} \\ \text{the same} \\ \text{as '}sr\text{'}}}$
   $= \mathbf{13pq - 5rs}$

Identities

$a + a + a = 3a$ and $a + 2a = 3a$ are both examples of identities and not equations, since **$3a$** is a different way of expressing **$a + a + a$** or **$a + 2a$**. In other words, what we have on the left-hand side of the equal sign is no different to what we have on the right-hand side of the equal sign. It is just written in a different way. The unknown (e.g. **a**) can take any value in an identity and it will always hold true.

Substitution

What is Substitution?

Substitution involves replacing the letters in a formula or expression with numbers and working out its value. This may involve working with positive or negative numbers, including fractions and decimals.

Examples

If $a = 3$, $b = 8$, $c = 20$ and $d = -4$, calculate the value of…

1 $2(a + b) - c$ Substitute in your numbers

$= 2(3 + 8) - 20$ Work out the bracket first

$= 2 \times 11 - 20$ Then the multiplication

$= 22 - 20$ Then the subtraction

$= 2$

2 $3d^2 + c$ Substitute in your numbers

$= 3 \times (-4)^2 + 20$ Work out the square first ($- \times - = +$)

$= 3 \times 16 + 20$ Then the multiplication

$= 48 + 20$ Then the addition

$= 68$

3 $\dfrac{c(d + 1)}{5}$ Substitute in your numbers

$= \dfrac{20(-4 + 1)}{5}$ Work out the bracket first

$= \dfrac{20 \times -3}{5}$ Then the multiplication ($+ \times - = -$)

$= \dfrac{-60}{5}$ Then the division ($- \div + = -$)

$= -12$

4 $\dfrac{1}{2}d^3$ Substitute in your numbers

$= \dfrac{1}{2} \times (-4)^3$ Work out the cube first ($- \times - = +$ and then $+ \times - = -$)

$= \dfrac{1}{2} \times -64$ Then the multiplication ($+ \times - = -$)

$= -32$

Some formulae are provided for you on a formulae sheet in the examination (see p.110). You may need to solve a problem by selecting the appropriate formula to use and substituting the given information.

Example

The diagram shows the positions of two coastguard stations, C1 and C2, from which a distress flare, F, is seen.

Calculate the distance of the distress flare from C1.

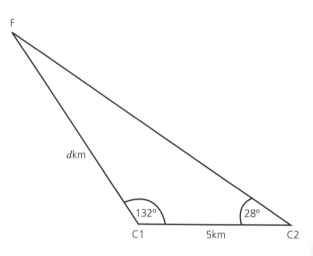

The appropriate formula to use in this case is the **sine rule** (see page 62).

Adapting the sine rule for this triangle gives

$$\frac{d}{\sin 28°} = \frac{5}{\sin F}$$

We need to find the size of angle F.

$$F = 180° - (132° + 28°) = 20°$$

$$\frac{d}{\sin 28°} = \frac{5}{\sin 20°}$$

$$d = \frac{5\sin 28°}{\sin 20°} = 6.863\ldots$$

The distance of the distress flare from C1 is 6.86km to 3 s.f.

Brackets and Factorisation

xy

Multiplying Out Brackets

When we multiply out a bracket, everything which is inside the bracket must be multiplied by whatever is immediately outside the bracket.

Examples

① $4(x + 3)$

$= 4 \times x + 4 \times 3$

$\mathbf{= 4x + 12}$

② $3x(4x^2 - 5)$

$= 3x \times 4x^2 + 3x \times \text{-}5$

$\mathbf{= 12x^3 - 15x}$

> If your expression includes two brackets, it may result in like terms, which you need to collect together and simplify.

③ $2(4x + 3) + 5(x - 2)$

$= 2 \times 4x + 2 \times 3 + 5 \times x + 5 \times \text{-}2$

$= 8x + 6 + 5x - 10$

$= 8x + 5x + 6 - 10$

    └─Like terms─┘ └─Like terms─┘

$\mathbf{= 13x - 4}$

④ $x(5 - x) + 4x(2x^2 + 3x)$

$= x \times 5 + x \times \text{-}x + 4x \times 2x^2 + 4x \times 3x$

$= 5x - x^2 + 8x^3 + 12x^2$

$= 8x^3 - x^2 + 12x^2 + 5x$

       └────Like terms────┘

$\mathbf{= 8x^3 + 11x^2 + 5x}$

> When you multiply out two brackets make sure that each term in the second bracket is multiplied by each term in the first bracket.

⑤ $(x + 2)(x + 3)$

$= x(x + 3) + 2(x + 3)$

$= x \times x + x \times 3 + 2 \times x + 2 \times 3$

$= x^2 + 3x + 2x + 6$

       └──Like terms──┘

$\mathbf{= x^2 + 5x + 6}$

⑥ $(3x - 2)^2$

$= (3x - 2)(3x - 2)$

$= 3x(3x - 2) - 2(3x - 2)$

$= 3x \times 3x + 3x \times \text{-}2 - 2 \times 3x - 2 \times \text{-}2$

$= 9x^2 - 6x - 6x + 4$

      └───Like terms───┘

$\mathbf{= 9x^2 - 12x + 4}$

Factorisation

Factorisation is the reverse process to multiplying out brackets. An expression is rewritten with a bracket by taking out highest common factors.

Examples

① $4x + 6 = \mathbf{2(2x + 3)}$

2 is the highest common factor of 4 and 6

② $6x^2 + 8x = \mathbf{2x(3x + 4)}$

$2x$ is the highest common factor of $6x^2$ and $8x$

③ $9x^3y^2 - 6xy^3 = \mathbf{3xy^2(3x^2 - 2y)}$

$3xy^2$ is the highest common factor of $9x^3y^2$ and $6xy^3$

④ $x(2y + 3) + z(2y + 3) = \mathbf{(2y + 3)(x + z)}$

$(2y + 3)$ is a common factor of $x(2y + 3)$ and $z(2y + 3)$

To check each of the examples above, multiply out each bracket. You should end up with the original expression.

Linear Equations

Linear Equations with the Unknown on One Side of the Equation

Equations such as…

$$4x = 12$$
$$x + 3 = 7$$
$$2(x + 5) = 14$$

… are all examples of linear equations since the highest power they contain is x^1 (i.e. x).

Each of these linear equations can be solved to find the 'unknown' value of x by collecting all the x's on one side and all the numbers on the other side. The simplest linear equation would involve one operation to solve it. Most however require at least two operations.

Examples

1 $\quad 6x = 15$

$$\frac{6x}{6} = \frac{15}{6}$$

$$x = 2.5$$

Divide both sides of the equation by **6** to leave just x on the left-hand side.

2 $\quad 3x - 5 = 19$

$$3x - 5 + 5 = 19 + 5$$

$$\frac{3x}{3} = \frac{24}{3}$$

$$x = 8$$

Add 5 to both sides of the equation to remove the **-5** from the left-hand side.

Divide both sides of the equation by **3** to leave just x on the left-hand side.

3 $\quad 18 = 4(x + 9)$

$$18 = 4x + 36$$

$$18 - 36 = 4x + 36 - 36$$

$$\frac{-18}{4} = \frac{4x}{4}$$

$$-4.5 = x$$

$$\text{or } x = -4.5$$

Multiply out the bracket on the right-hand side.

Subtract **36** from both sides of the equation to remove the **+36** on the right-hand side.

Divide both sides of the equation by **4** to leave just x on the right-hand side.

4 $\quad \dfrac{4x + 3}{3} + \dfrac{5x - 3}{4} = 8$

$$^4\cancel{12} \times \frac{(4x + 3)}{\cancel{3}} + ^3\cancel{12} \times \frac{(5x - 3)}{\cancel{4}} = 12 \times 8$$

$$16x + 12 + 15x - 9 = 96$$

$$31x + 3 = 96$$

$$31x + 3 - 3 = 96 - 3$$

$$\frac{31x}{31} = \frac{93}{31}$$

$$x = 3$$

Multiply all terms on both sides by **12**, which is the lowest common multiple of **3** and **4**, to remove the fractional values.

Collect like terms on the left-hand side of the equation.

Subtract **3** from both sides of the equation to remove the **+3** on the left-hand side.

Divide both sides of the equation by **31** to leave just x on the left-hand side.

Linear Equations

Linear Equations with the Unknown on Both Sides of the Equation

The following examples have the 'unknown', e.g. x, appearing on both sides of the equation. Once again they are solved by collecting all the x's on one side and all the numbers on the other side.

It does not really matter on which side of the equal sign you collect all the x's, it is your choice. In the examples below, they are collected on the side that has the most positive x's to start with. This ensures that you end up with a value for x rather than -x.

Examples

1

$$8x - 7 = 5x + 26$$

$$8x - 5x - 7 = 5x - 5x + 26$$ Subtract **5x** from both sides of the equation to leave all the **x**'s on the left-hand side.

$$3x - 7 + 7 = 26 + 7$$ Add **7** to both sides of the equation to remove the **-7** on the left-hand side.

$$\frac{3x}{3} = \frac{33}{3}$$ Divide both sides of the equation by **3** to leave just **x** on the left-hand side.

$$x = 11$$

2

$$4(3x - 2) = 15x + 22$$ Multiply out the bracket on the left-hand side.

$$12x - 8 = 15x + 22$$

$$12x - 12x - 8 = 15x - 12x + 22$$ Subtract **12x** from both sides of the equation to leave all the **x**'s on the right-hand side.

$$-8 - 22 = 3x + 22 - 22$$ Subtract **22** from both sides of the equation to remove the **22** on the right-hand side.

$$\frac{-30}{3} = \frac{3x}{3}$$ Divide both sides of the equation by **3** to leave just **x** on the right-hand side.

$$-10 = x$$
$$\text{or } x = -10$$

3

$$\frac{19 + x}{2} = 2 - x$$

$$2 \times \frac{19 + x}{2} = 2 \times (2 - x)$$ Multiply all terms on both sides by **2** to remove the fractional value.

$$19 + x = 4 - 2x$$

$$19 + x + 2x = 4 - 2x + 2x$$ Add **2x** to both sides of the equation to remove the -**2x** on the right-hand side.

$$19 - 19 + 3x = 4 - 19$$ Subtract **19** from both sides of the equation to remove the **19** on the left-hand side.

$$\frac{3x}{3} = \frac{-15}{3}$$ Divide both sides of the equation by **3** to leave just **x** on the right-hand side.

$$x = -5$$

Problem Solving Using Linear Equations

This involves being given information, forming a linear equation from the information given and then solving the equation.

Example

The four angles of a quadrilateral are: a, $a + 20°$, $a + 40°$ and $a + 60°$. Calculate the size of each angle.
We know that the angles of a quadrilateral add up to **360°**. Therefore…

$$a + (a + 20) + (a + 40) + (a + 60) = 360$$
$$4a + 120 = 360°$$
$$4a = 240° \quad \text{– Subtract 120 from both sides.}$$
$$a = 60° \quad \text{– Divide both sides by 4.}$$

$$a = 60°, a + 20° = 80°, a + 40° = 100°, a + 60° = 120°$$

Formulae

Changing the Subject of a Formula

Formulae show the relationship between two or more changeable quantities (variables). They can be written in words, but most often symbols are used instead.

For example, the area of a circle is given by the formula: $A = \pi r^2$, which describes the relationship between the area of a circle and its radius.

Formulae can be rearranged to make a different letter the 'subject', e.g. $a = b + c$ has a as the subject since it is on one side by itself. If we wanted to make b or c the subject then we would need to rearrange the formula by moving terms from one side of the equals sign to the other.

Examples

1 Make b the subject of the following formula.

$$a = b + c$$

$$a - c = b + \cancel{c} - \cancel{c}$$

or $b = a - c$

> Subtract c from both sides of the formula. This will remove the $+c$ on the right-hand side to leave b on its own.

> Rewrite the formula with b on the left-hand side.

2 Make x the subject of the following equation.

$$4(3x + 2y) = 5x + 2z$$

$$12x + 8y = 5x + 2z$$

$$12x - 5x + 8y = \cancel{5x} - \cancel{5x} + 2z$$

$$7x + \cancel{8y} - \cancel{8y} = 2z - 8y$$

$$\frac{\cancel{7}x}{\cancel{7}} = \frac{2z - 8y}{7}$$

$$x = \frac{2z - 8y}{7}$$

> Multiply out the bracket on the left-hand side.

> Subtract **5x** from both sides of the equation to remove the **5x** on the right-hand side.

> Subtract **8y** from both sides of the equation to remove the **+8y** on the left-hand side.

> Divide both sides of the equation by **7** to leave just x on the left-hand side.

3 Make g the subject of the following formula.

$$e = f + \frac{g}{d}$$

$$d \times e = d \times f + \cancel{d} \times \frac{g}{\cancel{d}}$$

$$de = df + g$$

$$de - df = \cancel{df} - \cancel{df} + g$$

$$g = de - df = d(e - f)$$

> Multiply all terms on both sides by d to remove the fractional value.

> Subtract df from both sides of the formula to leave just g on the right-hand side.

> Rewrite the formula with g on the left-hand side.

4 Make r the subject of the following formula.

$$A = \pi r^2$$

$$\frac{A}{\pi} = \frac{\cancel{\pi} r^2}{\cancel{\pi}}$$

$$\sqrt{\frac{A}{\pi}} = \sqrt{r^2}$$

$$\sqrt{\frac{A}{\pi}} = r \text{ or } r = \sqrt{\frac{A}{\pi}}$$

> Divide both sides of the formula by π to remove the π on the right-hand side

> Take the square root of both sides of the formula to remove the 'square' and leave just r on the right-hand side.

> Rewrite the formula with r on the left-hand side.

Formulae

xy

Using Formulae

Whenever you use a formula to work out an unknown quantity, all you are doing is substituting numbers for symbols.

Examples

1. The formula that converts a temperature reading from degrees Celsius (°C) into degrees Fahrenheit (°F) is…

$$F = \tfrac{9}{5}C + 32$$

What is the temperature in degrees Fahrenheit if the temperature in degrees Celsius is 25°C?

$F = \tfrac{9}{5} \times 25 + 32$ ← We substitute our value for C into the formula, to work out **F**

$F = 45 + 32$

F = 77°F

2. The area of a triangle is given by the formula:

$$A = \dfrac{b \times h}{2}$$

where **b** is length of base and **h** is height of triangle.

Calculate the height of a triangle of area 30cm² if the length of its base is 10cm.

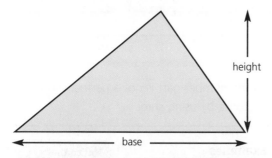

height

base

Since we want the subject of the formula to be **h**, we need to rearrange it.

$A \times 2 = \dfrac{b \times h}{\cancel{2}} \times \cancel{2}$ ← Multiply both sides by 2

$\dfrac{2A}{b} = \dfrac{\cancel{b} \times h}{\cancel{b}}$ ← Divide both sides by **b** to leave **h** on its own

$h = \dfrac{2A}{b}$

$h = \dfrac{2 \times 30}{10} = \dfrac{60}{10}$ ← We can now substitute in values for **A** and **b** to find **h**

h = 6cm

Generating Formulae

Generating a formulae, means writing a formula using given information. You may then need to use the formula to work out an unknown quantity.

Example

Generate a formula for the perimeter of a rectangle in terms of its area, **A**, and width, **w**, only. Use it to work out the perimeter of a rectangle of area 40cm² and width 4cm.

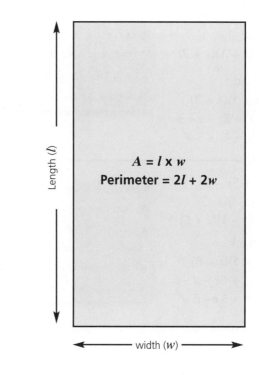

Length (*l*)

$A = l \times w$
Perimeter = $2l + 2w$

width (*w*)

$A = l \times w \longrightarrow l = \dfrac{A}{w}$

Firstly, we rearrange the formula for area to give us *l* on its own.

Perimeter = $2l + 2w$

… and then substitute for *l* in our formula for perimeter.

$= 2 \times \dfrac{A}{w} + 2w$

$= \dfrac{2A}{w} + 2w$ ← We now have a formula for perimeter in terms of area and width only. Therefore we can substitute in values for **A** and **w** to find the perimeter.

$= \dfrac{2 \times 40}{4} + 2 \times 4$

$= \dfrac{80}{4} + 8$

$= 20 + 8 = 28cm$

Quadratic Expressions

What is a Quadratic Expression?

A quadratic expression is an expression in which the highest power of x is x^2, e.g. $x^2 + 6x + 5$, $x^2 - 9$ or $x^2 - 3$. Quadratic expressions with terms that have no common factors give us two brackets when factorised, where each bracket contains a letter (usually x) and a number. To factorise a quadratic expression such as $x^2 + 6x + 5$ the quickest approach is to...

(1) Write out two brackets and put an x in each one...
$(x\ )(x\ )$

(2) Find two numbers which multiply to give the end number $+5 (+1 \times +5 = +5)$ and add up to give the middle number $+6 (+1 + +5 = +6)$

(3) Insert your numbers – one in each bracket. Therefore, $x^2 + 6x + 5 = (x + 1)(x + 5)$

Examples

1 $x^2 + 4x + 3$

$= (x\ )(x\ )$ ← Write out your two brackets and put an x in each one.

$= (x + 1)(x + 3)$ ← We now need two numbers that multiply to give $+3$ and also add up to $+4$.

$+1 \times +3 = +3$ ✓ and $+1 + +3 = +4$ ✓ (these are our two numbers)

$-1 \times -3 = +3$ ✓ and $-1 + -3 = -4$ ✗

Check:
$(x + 1)(x + 3)$
$= x^2 + 3x + x + 3$
$= x^2 + 4x + 3$ ✓

2 $x^2 + 5x - 6$

$= (x\ )(x\ )$ ← Write out your two brackets and put an x in each one.

$= (x - 1)(x + 6)$ ← We now need two numbers that multiply to give -6 and also add up to $+5$.

$+1 \times -6 = -6$ ✓ and $+1 + -6 = -5$ ✗

$-1 \times +6 = -6$ ✓ and $-1 + +6 = +5$ ✓ (these are our two numbers)

$+2 \times -3 = -6$ ✓ and $+2 + -3 = -1$ ✗

$-2 \times +3 = -6$ ✓ and $-2 + +3 = +1$ ✗

Check:
$(x - 1)(x + 6)$
$= x^2 + 6x - x - 6$
$= x^2 + 5x - 6$ ✓

When looking for our two numbers, it helps to remember:

$- \times - = +$ $- \times + = -$
$+ \times + = +$ $+ \times - = -$

Difference of Two Squares

There are some quadratic expressions that don't have any x's in the middle and end in – 'a number'^{2}, e.g. $x^2 - 1^2$, $x^2 - 2^2$, $x^2 - 3^2$, $x^2 - 4^2$. Expressions like these are known as the 'difference of two squares' and can be factorised. Again, you should check your answers by multiplying out the brackets – you should end up with the original expression.

Examples

1 $x^2 - 1 = x^2 - 1^2 = (x + 1)(x - 1)$

2 $x^2 - 4 = x^2 - 2^2 = (x + 2)(x - 2)$

3 $x^2 - 9 = x^2 - 3^2 = (x + 3)(x - 3)$ — This is why it is useful to learn the square numbers.

4 $x^2 - 16 = x^2 - 4^2 = (x + 4)(x - 4)$

When the number part is not a perfect square, you can still factorise by using surds.

Examples

$x^2 - 7 = (x + \sqrt{7})(x - \sqrt{7})$

$x^2 - 18 = (x + \sqrt{18})(x - \sqrt{18})$

Notice that
$\sqrt{18} = \sqrt{9 \times 2}$
$= \sqrt{9} \times \sqrt{2} = 3\sqrt{2}$
So $x^2 - 18$
$= (x + 3\sqrt{2})(x - 3\sqrt{2})$

The difference of two squares may also be used to simplify calculations.

Example

$81.6^2 - 18.4^2 = (81.6 + 18.4)(81.6 - 18.4)$

$= 100 \times 63.2$

$= 6320$

Quadratic Equations

Solving Quadratic Equations by Factorisation

Equations such as...

$x^2 + 4x + 3 = 0$

$x^2 - 16 = 0$

$2x^2 + 5x - 3 = 0$

... are all examples of quadratic equations (i.e. their highest power is x^2).

To solve a quadratic equation by factorisation:

(1) Rearrange the equation if necessary so that one side is equal to zero.

(2) Factorise the quadratic. **Note:** Not all quadratrics will factorise. In such cases you will need to use a different method such as completing the square or using a formula (see pp 34–35).

(3) Treat each bracket as a separate linear equation equal to 0 (zero).

The solution to quadratic equations may be shown graphically (see page 48).

Examples

1 $x^2 - 6x + 5 = 0$ ◄——

> To factorise the quadratic expression within the equation, we need two numbers that multiply to give **+5** and also add up to **-6**.
>
> $+1 \times +5 = +5$ ✓ and $+1 + +5 = +6$ ✗
>
> $-1 \times -5 = +5$ ✓ and $-1 + -5 = -6$ ✓ (these are our two numbers)

Our factorised quadratic equation now looks like...

$(x - 1)(x - 5) = 0$ ◄——

> • We now have two brackets which when multiplied together are equal to 0 (zero).
> • This is only possible if one or both of the two bracket is also equal to 0 (zero).
> • We now treat each bracket as a separate linear equation equal to 0 (zero).

And so...

$(x - 1) = 0$

$x - \cancel{1} + \cancel{1} = 0 + 1$

$x = 1$ ... is one solution

Check: $x = 1$

$x^2 - 6x + 5 = 0$

$1^2 - 6 \times 1 + 5 = 0$

$1 - 6 + 5 = 0$ ✓

or

$(x - 5) = 0$

$x - \cancel{5} + \cancel{5} = 0 + 5$

$x = 5$ ... is the other

Check: $x = 5$

$x^2 - 6x + 5 = 0$

$5^2 - 6 \times 5 + 5 = 0$

$25 - 30 + 5 = 0$ ✓

2 $x^2 - 5x - 14 = 0$ ◄——

> To factorise the quadratic expression within the equation, we need two numbers that multiply to give **-14** and also add up to **-5**.
>
> $+1 \times -14 = -14$ ✓ and $+1 + -14 = -13$ ✗
>
> $-1 \times +14 = -14$ ✓ and $-1 + +14 = +13$ ✗
>
> $+2 \times -7 = -14$ ✓ and $+2 + -7 = -5$ ✓ (these are our two numbers)
>
> $-2 \times +7 = -14$ ✓ and $-2 + +7 = +5$ ✗

Our factorised quadratic equation now looks like...

$(x + 2)(x - 7) = 0$

And so...

$(x + 2) = 0$

$x + \cancel{2} - \cancel{2} = 0 - 2$

$x = -2$ ... is one solution

Check: $x = -2$

$x^2 - 5x - 14 = 0$

$(-2)^2 - 5 \times -2 - 14 = 0$

$4 + 10 - 14 = 0$ ✓

or

$(x - 7) = 0$

$x - \cancel{7} + \cancel{7} = 0 + 7$

$x = 7$ ... is the other

Check: $x = 7$

$x^2 - 5x - 14 = 0$

$7^2 - 5 \times 7 - 14 = 0$

$49 - 35 - 14 = 0$ ✓

Quadratic Equations

Solving Quadratic Equations by Completing the Square

This is another method that can be used to solve quadratic equations and is particularly useful when the solutions are not integers. Although you can use this method, you should always try and factorise the quadratic expression within the quadratic equation first (as on page 33) in order to solve the equation.

1. Rearrange your equation so all the terms involving x^2 and x are on one side and your number is on the other side.
2. Write the terms in the form… $(x + \text{'number'})^2$ Your 'number' should have a value half that of the number before the term involving x.
2. Now expand the square bracket to get the original terms involving x^2 and x, **plus a new 'number'**. To balance the equation, add the new 'number' onto the other side too.
4. Take the square root of both sides of your equation to get two separate linear equations which you then solve.

Examples

1

$x^2 - 6x + 5 = 0$

$x^2 - 6x = -5$ — Rearrange your equation.

$(x - 3)^2 = -5 + 9$ — Complete the square and balance the equation by adding **+9** to the right-hand side.

$(x - 3)^2 = 4$

$\sqrt{(x-3)^2} = \sqrt{4}$ $[(x - 3)^2 = (x - 3)(x - 3) = x^2 - 6x + 9]$

$x - 3 = \pm 2$ — Take the square root of both sides.

We now have two separate linear equations:
$x - 3 = +2$ and $x - 3 = -2$

One solution…

$x - 3 = +2$

$x = 5$

Check:

$x^2 - 6x + 5 = 0$

$5^2 - 6 \times 5 + 5 = 0$

$25 - 30 + 5 = 0$ ✓

… or another solution

$x - 3 = -2$

$x = 1$

Check:

$x^2 - 6x + 5 = 0$

$1^2 - 6 \times 1 + 5 = 0$

$1 - 6 + 5 = 0$ ✓

2

$x^2 - 4x - 6 = 0$

$x^2 - 4x = 6$ — Rearrange your equation.

$(x - 2)^2 = 6 + 4$ — Complete the square and balance the equation by adding **+4** to the right-hand side.

$(x - 2)^2 = 10$ $[(x - 2)^2 = (x - 2)(x - 2) = x^2 - 4x + 4]$

$x - 2 = \pm\sqrt{10}$

$x - 2 = \pm 3.16$ — Take the square root of both sides.

We now have two separate linear equations:
$x - 2 = +3.16$ and $x - 2 = -3.16$

One solution…

$x - 2 = +3.16$

$x = 5.16$

Check:

$x^2 - 4x - 6 = 0$

$(5.16)^2 - (4 \times 5.16) - 6 = 0$

$26.63 - 20.64 - 6 = 0$ ✓

… or another solution

$x - 2 = -3.16$

$x = -1.16$

Check:

$x^2 - 4x - 6 = 0$

$(-1.16)^2 - (4 \times -1.16) - 6 = 0$

$1.35 + 4.64 - 6 = 0$ ✓

Quadratic Equations

Solving Quadratic Equations by Using the Formula

This formula can be used to solve quadratic equations:

$$x = \frac{-b \pm \sqrt{b^2 - 4ac}}{2a}$$

This method is again useful when the solutions are not whole numbers. It can be used to solve equations in the form $ax^2 + bx + c = 0$

Examples

1 $x^2 - 6x + 5 = 0$

In this case, **$a = 1$, $b = -6$** and **$c = 5$**. If we now substitute these values into the formula:

$$x = \frac{-b \pm \sqrt{b^2 - 4ac}}{2a}$$

$$x = \frac{6 \pm \sqrt{(-6)^2 - (4 \times 1 \times 5)}}{2 \times 1}$$

$$x = \frac{6 \pm \sqrt{36 - 20}}{2}$$

$$x = \frac{6 \pm \sqrt{16}}{2}$$

$$x = \frac{6 \pm 4}{2}$$

> We now have two separate linear equations:

One solution…

$$x = \frac{6 + 4}{2}$$

$$x = \frac{10}{2}$$

$$x = 5$$

Check:

$x^2 - 6x + 5 = 0$
$(5)^2 - (6 \times 5) + 5 = 0$
$25 - 30 + 5 = 0$ ✓

… or another solution

$$x = \frac{6 - 4}{2}$$

$$x = \frac{2}{2}$$

$$x = 1$$

Check:

$x^2 - 6x + 5 = 0$
$(1)^2 - (6 \times 1) + 5 = 0$
$1 - 6 + 5 = 0$ ✓

2 $5x^2 + 2x - 4 = 0$

Therefore, **$a = 5$, $b = 2$** and **$c = -4$**. If we now substitute these values into the formula:

$$x = \frac{-b \pm \sqrt{b^2 - 4ac}}{2a}$$

$$x = \frac{-2 \pm \sqrt{(2)^2 - (4 \times 5 \times -4)}}{2 \times 5}$$

$$x = \frac{-2 \pm \sqrt{4 + 80}}{10}$$

$$x = \frac{-2 \pm \sqrt{84}}{10}$$

$$x = \frac{-2 \pm 9.165}{10}$$

> We now have two separate linear equations:

One solution…

$$x = \frac{-2 + 9.165}{10}$$

$$x = \frac{7.165}{10}$$

$$x = 0.72 \text{ (to 2 d.p.)}$$

Check:

$5x^2 + 2x - 4 = 0$
$5 \times (0.72)^2 + (2 \times 0.72) - 4 = 0$
$2.59 + 1.44 - 4 = 0$ ✓

… or another solution

$$x = \frac{-2 - 9.165}{10}$$

$$x = \frac{-11.165}{10}$$

$$x = -1.12 \text{ (to 2 d.p.)} \quad \text{(allowing for rounding errors)}$$

Check:

$5x^2 + 2x - 4 = 0$
$5 \times (-1.12)^2 + (2 \times -1.12) - 4 = 0$
$6.27 - 2.24 - 4 = 0$ ✓

Trial and Improvement

Solving Equations by Trial and Improvement

This method can be used to find a solution to any equation. As the name suggests, we trial a possible solution by substituting its value into the equation.

The process is then repeated using a different possible solution and so on. The idea is that each subsequent trial is an improvement on the previous trial.

Examples

1. The equation $x^3 + x = 20$ has a solution somewhere between $x = 2$ and $x = 3$. By trial and improvement, calculate a solution to the equation to 2 decimal places.

Since we are told that there is a solution between $x = 2$ and $x = 3$ we will substitute their values into our equation to see what $x^3 + x$ gives us. Remember we want its value to be equal to **20**.

x	$x^3 + x$	Comment
2	$2^3 + 2 = 8 + 2 = \mathbf{10}$	Less than 20
3	$3^3 + 3 = 27 + 3 = \mathbf{30}$	More than 20
Try 2.5	$2.5^3 + 2.5 = 15.625 + 2.5 = \mathbf{18.125}$	Less than 20
Try 2.6	$2.6^3 + 2.6 = 17.576 + 2.6 = \mathbf{20.176}$	More than 20
Try 2.55	$2.55^3 + 2.55 = 16.581375 + 2.55 = \mathbf{19.131375}$	Less than 20
Try 2.58	$2.58^3 + 2.58 = 17.173512 + 2.58 = \mathbf{19.753512}$	Less than 20
Try 2.59	$2.59^3 + 2.59 = 17.373979 + 2.59 = \mathbf{19.963979}$	Less than 20
Try 2.595	$2.595^3 + 2.595 = 17.474795 + 2.595 = \mathbf{20.069795}$	Just more than 20

So $x = \mathbf{2.59}$ (to 2 d.p.) since the last trial above ($x = \mathbf{2.595}$) is more than 20.

If the last trial had been less than 20 then $x = \mathbf{2.60}$ (to 2 d.p.) would be the solution. (It is important to try the middle value (**2.595**)).

2. The equation $x^2 - \frac{12}{x} = 10$ has a solution somewhere between $x = 3$ and $x = 4$.

By trial and improvement, calculate a solution to the equation to 2 decimal places.

x	$x^2 - \frac{12}{x}$	Comment
3	$3^2 - \frac{12}{3} = 9 - 4 = \mathbf{5}$	Less than 10
4	$4^2 - \frac{12}{4} = 16 - 3 = \mathbf{13}$	More than 10
Try 3.5	$3.5^2 - \frac{12}{3.5} = 12.25 - 3.4285714 = \mathbf{8.8214286}$	Less than 10
Try 3.6	$3.6^2 - \frac{12}{3.6} = 12.96 - 3.3333333 = \mathbf{9.6266667}$	Less than 10
Try 3.7	$3.7^2 - \frac{12}{3.7} = 13.69 - 3.2432432 = \mathbf{10.446757}$	More than 10
Try 3.65	$3.65^2 - \frac{12}{3.65} = 13.3225 - 3.2876712 = \mathbf{10.034829}$	More than 10
Try 3.64	$3.64^2 - \frac{12}{3.64} = 13.2496 - 3.2967033 = \mathbf{9.9528967}$	Less than 10
Try 3.645	$3.645^2 - \frac{12}{3.645} = 13.286025 - 3.2921811 = \mathbf{9.9938439}$	Just less than 10

So $x = \mathbf{3.65}$ (to 2 d.p.) since the last trial above ($x = \mathbf{3.645}$) is less than 10.

If the last trial had been more than 10 then $x = \mathbf{3.64}$ (to 2 d.p.) would be the solution. (It is important to try the middle value (**3.645**)).

Sequences

Number Patterns and Sequences

A number pattern or sequence is a series of numbers which follow a rule. Each number in a sequence is called a **term**, where the first number in the sequence is called the **1st term** and so on.

Examples

1st term	2nd term	3rd term	4th term		The next two terms

① 2,   6,   10,   14,...
+4   +4   +4

> The rule is that each term is **4 more** than the previous term. These terms have a common difference of +4

...18,   22, ...
+4

② 20,   17,   14,   11,...
-3   -3   -3

> The rule is that each term is **3 less** than the previous term. These terms have a common difference of -3

... 8,   5, ...
-3

③ 1,   3,   9,   27,...
×3   ×3   ×3

> The rule is that each term is **3 times** the previous term. These terms don't have a common difference between them

...81,   243,...
×3

A sequence can also be a series of diagrams.

④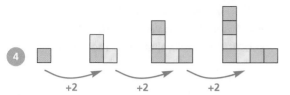
+2   +2   +2

> Each diagram (term) has **2 more** boxes in it than the previous diagram. These diagrams have a common difference of +2

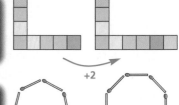
+2

⑤
+1   +1   +1

> Each diagram (term) has **1 more** match in it than the previous diagram. These diagrams have a common difference of +1

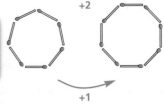
+1

Other Examples

① Squared integers

1,   4,   9,   16,...
(1² = 1) (2² = 4) (3² = 9) (4² = 16)

② Triangular numbers

1,   3,   6,   10,...
+2   +3   +4

③ Powers of 2

1,   2,   4,   8, ...
(2⁰ = 1) (2¹ = 2) (2² = 4) (2³ = 8)

④ Powers of 10

1,   10,   100, 1000,...
(10⁰ = 1) (10¹ = 10) (10² = 100) (10³ = 1000)

Sequences

The nth Term of a Sequence

The nth term is a formula which enables us to generate any term within a particular sequence.

Example

Let our sequence of numbers have an **nth term = $2n + 2$** where n is the position of the term, i.e. the first term has $n = 1$, the second term has $n = 2$ and so on. This formula now enables us to generate any term simply by substituting our value for n into the formula.

nth term $= 2n + 2$
1st term $= 2 \times 1 + 2 = 4$
2nd term $= 2 \times 2 + 2 = 6$
3rd term $= 2 \times 3 + 2 = 8$
4th term $= 2 \times 4 + 2 = 10$
100th term $= 2 \times 100 + 2 = 202$

So, our sequence of numbers would look like…
4, 6, 8, 10, …

Finding the nth term of an Arithmetic Sequence

A sequence where there is a common difference between the terms can be described by a linear algebraic expression. The general formula for the nth term of these sequences is…

---

nth term = $an + b$

where a is the common difference between the terms and b is a constant.

The first thing you do is determine the value of a. To then find b substitute the value for the 1st term, $n = 1$ and a into the formula.

Examples

①

These terms have a common difference of **+2** and so $a = 2$. If we take the 1st term then $n = 1$ and it has a value of **5**. We then substitute these values into the formula…

nth term $= an + b$
$5 = 2 \times 1 + b$

$b = 5 - 2$
$\quad = 3$

Therefore **nth term = $2n + 3$**

To check:
2nd term $= 2 \times 2 + 3 = 4 + 3 = 7$ ✓
3rd term $= 2 \times 3 + 3 = 6 + 3 = 9$ ✓

② **20,   17,   14,   11,…**
$\quad$ -3 $\quad$ -3 $\quad$ -3

These terms have a common difference of **-3** and so $a = -3$. If we take the 1st term then $n = 1$ and it has a value of **20**. We then substitute these values into the formula…

nth term $= an + b$
$20 = -3 \times 1 + b$

$b = 20 + 3$
$\quad = 23$

Therefore **nth term = $-3n + 23$**

To check:
2nd term $= -3 \times 2 + 23 = -6 + 23 = 17$ ✓
3rd term $= -3 \times 3 + 23 = -9 + 23 = 14$ ✓

Straight Line Graphs

Graphs of Linear Functions

A linear function, e.g. $y = x$, $y = 2x - 1$, $y = 0.5x + 1$, (i.e. a function that may be written in the form $ax + b$, where a and b are constants), will always give you a straight line graph when drawn.

To draw the graph of a linear function you only need to plot three points.

Examples

1 Draw the graph of $y = 2x - 1$ for values of x between **-2** and **2** (this may be written $-2 \leqslant x \leqslant 2$).

Firstly, we need to pick at least 3 values of x, within the range, so that we can work out their y values. The two extreme values of x and one in the middle will do. Draw a table of results as follows:

Table of results for $y = 2x - 1$

x	-2	0	2
$2x$	(2 × -2 =) -4	(2 × 0 =) 0	(2 × 2 =) 4
-1	-1	-1	-1
$y = 2x - 1$	(-4 − 1 =) **-5**	(0 − 1 =) **-1**	(4 − 1 =) **3**

We now have the coordinates of 3 points – (-2,-5), (0,-1) and (2,3) – and can plot our graph.

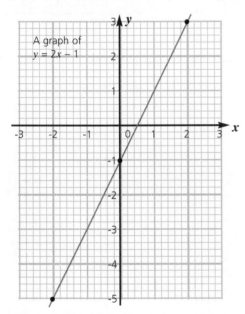

A graph of $y = 2x - 1$

Remember your straight line must pass through all 3 points! If it doesn't then one of your points is wrong. You can either check your table again or, better still, work out the coordinates of another point, e.g. when $x = $ **-1** or $x = $ **1**.

2 Draw the graph of $2y + x = 4$ for values of between **-2** and **2**.

The first thing we have to do is rearrange the function to make y the subject. When we have done that we can draw a table of results.

$$2y + x = 4$$
$$2y + x - x = -x + 4$$
$$\frac{2y}{2} = \frac{-x}{2} + \frac{4}{2}$$

Subtract x from both sides

Divide both sides by 2

To give us... $y = -0.5x + 2$

Table of results for $y = -0.5x + 2$

x	-2	0	2
$-0.5x$	(-0.5 × -2 =) 1	(-0.5 × 0 =) 0	(-0.5 × 2 =) -1
+ 2	+2	+2	+2
$y = -0.5x + 2$	(1 + 2 =) **3**	(0 + 2 =) **2**	(-1 + 2 =) **1**

We now have the coordinates of 3 points – (-2,3), (0,2) and (2,1) – and can plot our graph.

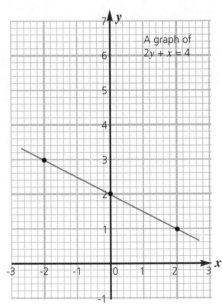

A graph of $2y + x = 4$

Gradients

$y = mx + c$

The general equation of any line **not** parallel to the y-axis may be written in the form $y = mx + c$ where…

- m is the value of the gradient. The gradient or slope of a line is a measure of the steepness of the line; the bigger the gradient the steeper the line. The gradient of a line can either be positive or negative, depending on which way the line slopes.

- c is the value of the intercept. The intercept of a line is simply the y value at the point where the line crosses the y-axis.

Each of the graphs below have the same intercept ($c = +1$) but different gradients. The gradient of the lines in graph ① and ② are both positive with graph ② having a steeper slope ($m = 3$ as compared to $m = 2$ for graph ②). The line in graph ③ has a negative gradient ($m = -2$) and so it slopes in the opposite direction to the other two graphs.

Remember, a positive (+) gradient goes **up** from left to right (as we read) whereas a negative (-) gradient goes **down** from left to right.

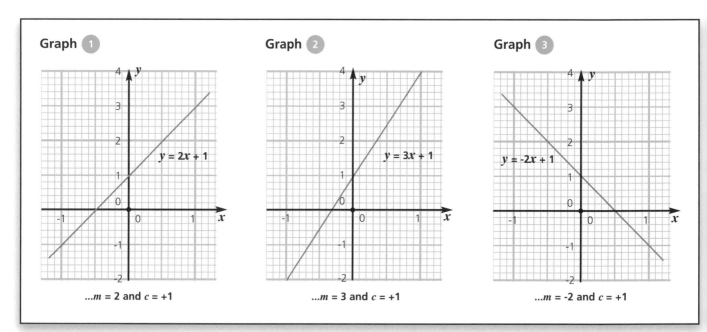

Graph ①

$y = 2x + 1$

…$m = 2$ and $c = +1$

Graph ②

$y = 3x + 1$

…$m = 3$ and $c = +1$

Graph ③

$y = -2x + 1$

…$m = -2$ and $c = +1$

Gradients of Parallel Lines

Lines represented by equations that have the same gradient will be parallel even if each equation has a different intercept, for example, lines represented by $y = 2x + 2$ and $y = 2x - 1$ are parallel.

Example

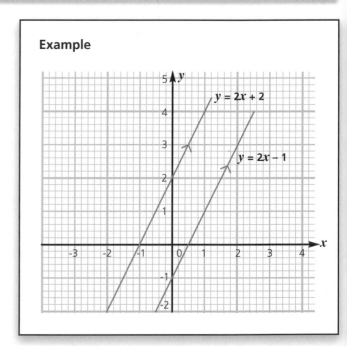

$y = 2x + 2$

$y = 2x - 1$

Linear Inequalities

xy

Four Kinds of Inequality

1 **>** which means 'Greater than'

e.g. if $x > 4$ then x can have any value 'greater than' **4** but it can't have a value equal to **4**.

This inequality can be shown using a number line. An open ○ circle means that $x = 4$ is not included in the inequality.

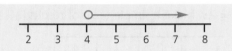

2 **⩾** which means 'Greater than or Equal to'

e.g. if $x ⩾ 4$ then x can have any value 'greater than' **4** and its value can also be 'equal to' **4**.

This inequality can be shown using a number line. A closed ● circle means that $x = 4$ is included in the inequality.

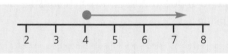

3 **<** which means 'Less than'

e.g. if $x < 1$ then x can have any value 'less than' **1** but it can't have a value equal to **1**.

This inequality can be shown using a number line. An open ○ circle means that $x = 1$ is not included in the inequality.

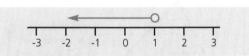

4 **⩽** which means 'Less than or Equal to'

e.g. if $x ⩽ 1$ then x can have any value 'less than' **1** and its value can also be 'equal to' **1**.

This inequality can be shown using a number line. A closed ● circle means that $x = 1$ is included in the inequality.

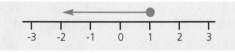

Number lines can also be used to show a combination of inequalities.

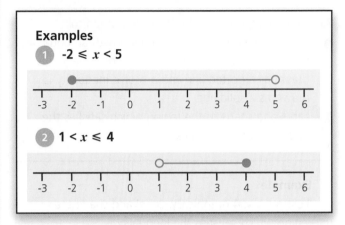

Examples

1 $-2 ⩽ x < 5$

2 $1 < x ⩽ 4$

Solving Linear Inequalities

Solving these is just like solving linear equations except we have an inequality sign instead of the equal sign.

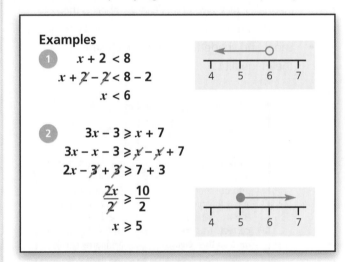

Examples

1
$x + 2 < 8$
$x + \cancel{2} - \cancel{2} < 8 - 2$
$x < 6$

2
$3x - 3 ⩾ x + 7$
$3x - x - 3 ⩾ \cancel{x} - \cancel{x} + 7$
$2x - \cancel{3} + \cancel{3} ⩾ 7 + 3$
$\dfrac{\cancel{2}x}{\cancel{2}} ⩾ \dfrac{10}{2}$
$x ⩾ 5$

However, if you multiply or divide an inequality by a negative number then you must always reverse the direction of the inequality sign.

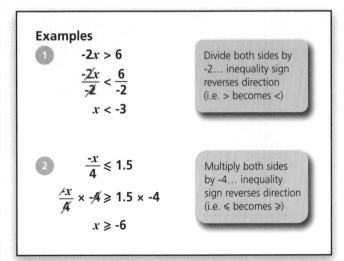

Examples

1
$-2x > 6$
$\dfrac{\cancel{-2}x}{\cancel{-2}} < \dfrac{6}{-2}$
$x < -3$

Divide both sides by -2... inequality sign reverses direction (i.e. > becomes <)

2
$\dfrac{-x}{4} ⩽ 1.5$
$\dfrac{\cancel{-}x}{\cancel{4}} \times \cancel{-4} ⩾ 1.5 \times -4$
$x ⩾ -6$

Multiply both sides by -4... inequality sign reverses direction (i.e. ⩽ becomes ⩾)

Linear Inequalities

Illustrating Linear Inequalities Graphically

Any linear inequality can be illustrated graphically:

1. Treat the inequality as an equation with an equal (=) sign and draw its graph where a > or < inequality is drawn as a dotted line and a ⩾ or ⩽ inequality is drawn as a solid line.
2. Label and shade in the region which satisfies the inequality or inequalities.

Example

Illustrate $x < 4$ graphically. Label and shade the region which satisfies the inequality.

- Firstly draw the graph of $x = 4$ (remember to draw a dotted line).
- To determine the region which satisfies the inequality, pick two points (we've labelled them A and B) one on each side of the line $x = 4$ (see graph).
- Label and shade the region which satisfies the inequality.

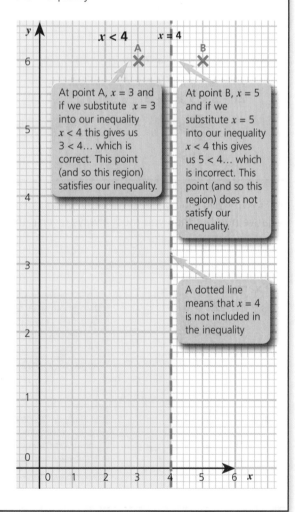

At point A, $x = 3$ and if we substitute $x = 3$ into our inequality $x < 4$ this gives us $3 < 4$... which is correct. This point (and so this region) satisfies our inequality.

At point B, $x = 5$ and if we substitute $x = 5$ into our inequality $x < 4$ this gives us $5 < 4$... which is incorrect. This point (and so this region) does not satisfy our inequality.

A dotted line means that $x = 4$ is not included in the inequality

Representing Linear Inequalities in Two Variables

Example

Illustrate $y ⩾ 1$, $y < 2x$ and $x + y ⩽ 6$ graphically. Label and shade the single region that is satisfied by all of these inequalities.

Draw the graph of...

... $y = 1$

... $y = 2x$. Make a simple table of results.

x	0	2	4
$y = 2x$	0	4	8

... $x + y = 6$. Rearrange to give y on its own and make a simple table of results.

x	0	3	6
$y = 6 - x$	6	3	0

Label and shade the region which satisfies all three inequalities.

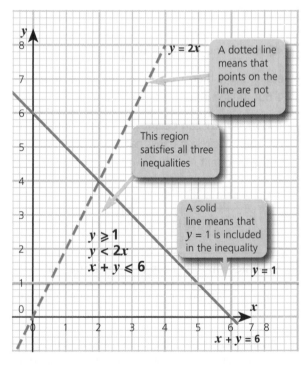

$y = 2x$

A dotted line means that points on the line are not included

This region satisfies all three inequalities

A solid line means that $y = 1$ is included in the inequality

$y ⩾ 1$
$y < 2x$
$x + y ⩽ 6$

$y = 1$

$x + y = 6$

Note: You may be asked to shade the 'unwanted region', particularly when representing several inequalities on the same diagram. The region left unshaded in this case will be the region that satisfies all of the inequalities.

Simultaneous Equations

xy

Solving Simultaneous Equations by Elimination

Simultaneous equations are where you work with two related equations (e.g. where x and y represent the same thing in both equations) at the same time. Individually the equations do not provide enough information for you to solve them (i.e. to find the values of x and y). However, when you work with both of them 'simultaneously' they provide enough combined information to solve them.

To solve simultaneous equations we need both equations to have the same coefficients (numbers in front of the unknown values, e.g. x and y).
- If these two numbers have the same sign (i.e. both positive or both negative) then we subtract one equation from the other.
- If these two numbers have different signs (i.e. one is positive and one is negative) then we add the two equations together.

Examples

① Solve the two simultaneous equations:
$4x + 2y = 14$ and $x + 2y = 8$

> Label the equations ① and ②

$$4x + 2y = 14 \quad ①$$
$$x + 2y = 8 \quad ②$$

> Equations ① and ② both have the same number of y's with the same sign (+), so we subtract one equation from the other to remove the y's.

Subtract ① − ②
$$4x + 2y = 14 \quad ①$$
$$- (x + 2y = 8) \quad ②$$
$$\overline{3x \quad\quad = 6}$$
To give us: $x = 2$

> To find the value of y, substitute $x = 2$ back into equation ① or ② (pick the easiest).
> If we take equation ② ...

$$x + 2y = 8$$
$$2 + 2y = 8$$
$$2y = 8 - 2$$
$$2y = 6$$
$$y = 3$$

> To check our solutions substitute $x = 2$ and $y = 3$ into equation ① since we used equation ② to find the value of y.

$4x + 2y = 14$
$4 \times 2 + 2 \times 3 = 14$
$8 + 6 = 14$ and that's correct. ✓

② Solve the two simultaneous equations:
$2p + 3q = 13$ and $3p - q = 3$

> Label the equations ① and ②

$$2p + 3q = 13 \quad ①$$
$$3p - q = 3 \quad ②$$

> Multiply equation ② by 3 so that this equation now has the same number of q's as equation ①. Equation ② now becomes equation ③.

② × 3 ⟶ $9p - 3q = 9 \quad ③$

> Equations ① and ③ now have the same number of q's but with different signs so we add the two equations together to remove the q's.

Add ① + ③
$$2p + 3q = 13 \quad ①$$
$$+ (9p - 3q = 9) \quad ③$$
$$\overline{11p \quad\quad = 22}$$
To give us: $p = 2$

> To find the value of q, substitute $p = 2$ into equation ①, ② or ③. If we take the equation ① ...

$$2p + 3q = 13$$
$$2 \times 2 + 3q = 13$$
$$3p = 13 - 4$$
$$3p = 9$$
$$q = 3$$

> To check our solutions substitute $p = 2$ and $q = 3$ into equation ② or ③ since we used equation ① to find the value of q. If we take equation ② ...

$3p - q = 3$
$3 \times 2 - 3 = 3$
$6 - 3 = 3$ and that's correct. ✓

Simultaneous Equations

Solving Linear Simultaneous Equations Graphically

Simultaneous equations can also be solved graphically. Linear equations when plotted give us straight line graphs. At the point of intersection the corresponding x and y values are the solutions of the simultaneous equations.

If the lines are parallel then there is no point of intersection and the equations cannot be solved simultaneously, e.g. $x + y = 6$ and $x + y = 4$.

Examples

1 Solve graphically the two simultaneous equations $x + y = 5$ and $2x + y = 7$ where the value of x lies in the range $1 \leqslant x \leqslant 5$ (i.e. somewhere between **1** and **5**).

> For each equation we need 3 corresponding values of x and y which can then be plotted so that we can draw our graph. This may mean rearranging an equation to give us y on its own.

Our First Equation

$x + y = 5$
$\therefore y = 5 - x$

x	1	3	5
$y = 5 - x$	$(5-1=)$ **4**	$(5-3=)$ **2**	$(5-5=)$ **0**

Our Second Equation

$2x + y = 7$
$\therefore y = 7 - 2x$

x	1	3	5
$y = 7 - 2x$	$(7-2\times1=)$ **5**	$(7-2\times3=)$ **1**	$(7-2\times5=)$ **-3**

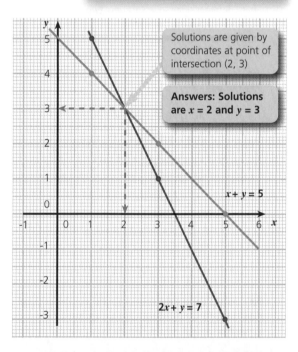

> Solutions are given by coordinates at point of intersection (2, 3)

> **Answers: Solutions are $x = 2$ and $y = 3$**

> To check our solutions substitute $x = 2$ and $y = 3$ into our two equations: $x + y = 5$: $2 + 3 = 5$ ✓ and $2x + y = 7$: $2 \times 2 + 3 = 7$: $4 + 3 = 7$ ✓

2 Solve graphically the two simultaneous equations $4x = y + 3$ and $2x + 2y = 9$ where the value of x lies in the range $0 \leqslant x \leqslant 2$ (i.e. somewhere between **0** and **2**).

Our First Equation

$4x = y + 3$
$y = 4x - 3$

x	0	1	2
$y = 4x - 3$	$(4\times0-3=)$ **-3**	$(4\times1-3=)$ **1**	$(4\times2-3=)$ **5**

Our Second Equation

$2x + 2y = 9$
$2y = 9 - 2x$
$y = \dfrac{9 - 2x}{2}$

x	0	1	2
$y = \dfrac{9-2x}{2}$	$\left(\dfrac{9-2\times0}{2}\right)=$ **4.5**	$\left(\dfrac{9-2\times1}{2}\right)=$ **3.5**	$\left(\dfrac{9-2\times2}{2}\right)=$ **2.5**

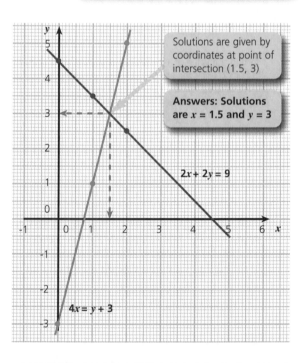

> Solutions are given by coordinates at point of intersection (1.5, 3)

> **Answers: Solutions are $x = 1.5$ and $y = 3$**

> To check our solutions substitute $x = 1.5$ and $y = 3$ into our two equations: $4x = y + 3$: $4 \times 1.5 = 3 + 3$: $6 = 3 + 3$ ✓ and $2x + 2y = 9$: $2 \times 1.5 + 2 \times 3 = 9$: $3 + 6 = 9$ ✓

Simultaneous Equations

xy

Solving Simultaneous Linear and Quadratic Equations

You are also expected to be able to use elimination to solve two simultaneous equations with two unknowns (i.e. x and y), where one equation is linear in each unknown (e.g. $y = 7x - 6$, $2x + y = 11$) and the other equation is linear in one unknown and quadratic in the other (e.g. $y = 3x^2$), or is of the form $x^2 + y^2 = r^2$ (e.g. $x^2 + y^2 = 25$ which is the same as $x^2 + y^2 = 5^2$).

$x^2 + y^2 = r^2$ is the equation of a circle of radius r, centred at the origin (0,0).

Examples

1 Solve the two simultaneous equations:
   $y = 7x + 6$ and $y = 3x^2$

> Label the equations ① and ②

$$y = 7x + 6 \quad ①$$
$$y = 3x^2 \quad ②$$

> Since both equations have y on its own as the subject, substitute y from equation ② into equation ①. Doing this will remove y from equation ①.

$$3x^2 = 7x + 6$$
$$3x^2 - 7x - 6 = 0$$

> What we have now is a quadratic equation. Always solve by factorisation if possible (see page 27). However you can solve by completing the square or by using the quadratic formula if necessary.

$$3x^2 - 7x - 6 = 0$$
$$(x - 3)(3x + 2) = 0$$

And so... $x - 3 = 0$
$$x = 3$$

or... $3x + 2 = 0$
$$x = \frac{-2}{3}$$

> To find the value of y, (when $x = 3$) substitute $x = 3$ into equation ①...

$$y = 7x + 6$$
$$y = (7 \times 3) + 6 = 27$$
One pair of solutions is $x = 3$ and $y = 27$

> To find the value of y (when $x = \frac{-2}{3}$) substitute $x = \frac{-2}{3}$ into equation ① or ②. If we take equation ①...

$$y = 7x + 6$$
$$y = (7 \times \frac{-2}{3}) + 6 = 1\frac{1}{3}$$

The other pair of solutions is $x = \frac{-2}{3}$ and $y = 1\frac{1}{3}$

> Always check your solutions by substituting them into equation ② since we used equation ① to find them.

2 Solve the two simultaneous equations:
   $2x + y = 11$ and $x^2 + y^2 = 25$

> Label the equations ① and ②

$$2x + y = 11 \quad ①$$
$$x^2 + y^2 = 25 \quad ②$$

> Rearrange equation ① to make y the subject.

$$y = 11 - 2x$$

> We can now substitute y from equation ① into equation ②. Doing this will remove y from equation ②.

$$x^2 + (11 - 2x)^2 = 25$$
$$x^2 + (11 - 2x)(11 - 2x) = 25$$
$$x^2 + 121 - 22x - 22x + 4x^2 = 25$$
$$x^2 + 4x^2 - 22x - 22x + 121 - 25 = 0$$
$$5x^2 - 44x + 96 = 0$$
$$(x - 4)(5x - 24) = 0$$

And so... $x - 4 = 0$
$$x = 4$$

> To get y, substitute $x = 4$ into rearranged equation ①.

$$y = 11 - 2x$$
$$y = 11 - (2 \times 4) = 3$$
One pair of solutions is $x = 4$ and $y = 3$.

or... $5x - 24 = 0$
$$5x = 24$$
$$x = \frac{24}{5} = 4.8$$

> To get y, substitute $x = 4.8$ into rearranged equation ①.

$$y = 11 - 2x$$
$$y = 11 - (2 \times 4.8) = 1.4$$
The other pair of solutions is $x = 4.8$ and $y = 1.4$

> Always check your solutions by substituting them into equation ② since we used equation ① to find them.

Simultaneous Equations

Solving Simultaneous Linear and Quadratic Equations Graphically

Approximate solutions to simultaneous linear and quadratic equations can also be found graphically. When drawn there are two points of intersection (there are exceptions, see Note) to give us two pairs of solutions.

Examples

1 Solve graphically the two simultaneous equations $y - x = 4$ and $y = 2x^2$ where the value of x lies in the range $-2 \leqslant x \leqslant 2$.

Our First Equation

$y - x = 4$
$\therefore y = x + 4$

x	-2	0	2
$y = x + 4$	2	4	6

Our Second Equation

$y = 2x^2$
(see next page)

x	-2	-1	0	1	2
$y = 2x^2$	8	2	0	2	8

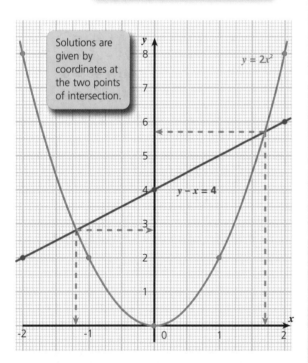

Solutions are given by coordinates at the two points of intersection.

One pair of solutions is $x = -1.2$ and $y = 2.8$
The other pair of solutions is $x = 1.7$ and $y = 5.7$

Remember to check your solutions by substituting the values of x and y into your two equations.

2 Solve graphically the two simultaneous equations $x + y = -1$ and $x^2 + y^2 = 9$ where the value of x lies in the range $-3 \leqslant x \leqslant 3$.

Our First Equation

$x + y = -1$
$\therefore y = -x - 1$

x	-3	0	3
$y = -x - 1$	2	-1	-4

Our Second Equation

The equation is $x^2 + y^2 = 9$ or $x^2 + y^2 = 3^2$, i.e. the equation of a circle of radius 3 units centred at the origin (0,0).

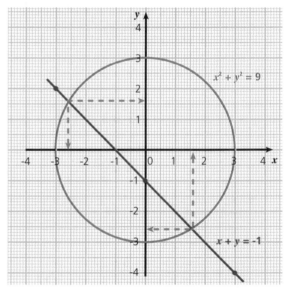

N.B. It is possible to get only one pair of solutions. This would occur if the line was a tangent to the curve or circle.

One pair of solutions is $x = -2.6$ and $y = 1.6$
The other pair of solutions is $x = 1.6$ and $y = -2.6$

Remember to check your solutions by substituting the values of x and y into your two equations.

Graphs of Quadratic Functions

Drawing Graphs of Quadratic Functions

A quadratic function is one that can be put in the form $y = ax^2 + bx + c$. Examples would include $y = x^2$, $y = x^2 - 5$, $y = x^2 - 2x$, $y = x^2 + 4$. These functions always produce a curved graph such as the ones below. To draw a curved graph we need to plot a **full range of points** as this increases the accuracy of our curve (compare this with straight line graphs).

Examples

1 Draw the graph of $y = x^2$ for values of x between **-3** and **3** ($-3 \leqslant x \leqslant 3$).

Table of results for $y = x^2$

x	-3	-2	-1	0	1	2	3
$y = x^2$	$(-3)^2=$ 9	$(-2)^2=$ 4	$(-1)^2=$ 1	$(0)^2=$ 0	$(1)^2=$ 1	$(2)^2=$ 4	$(3)^2=$ 9

We now have the coordinates of 7 points, so we can draw our graph.

Remember… your curve must be smooth and it must pass through all of the points plotted.

2 Draw the graph of $y = x^2 - 2x - 2$ for values of x between **-2** and **4** ($-2 \leqslant x \leqslant 4$).

Table of results for $y = x^2 - 2x - 2$

x	-2	-1	0	1	2	3	4
x^2	$(-2)^2=$ 4	$(-1)^2=$ 1	$(0)^2=$ 0	$(1)^2=$ 1	$(2)^2=$ 4	$(3)^2=$ 9	$(4)^2=$ 16
$-2x$	-2×-2= +4	-2×-1= +2	-2×0= 0	-2×1= -2	-2×2= -4	-2×3= -6	-2×4= -8
-2	-2	-2	-2	-2	-2	-2	-2
$y = x^2 - 2x - 2$	6	1	-2	-3	-2	1	6

Again we have the coordinates of 7 points, so we can draw our graph.

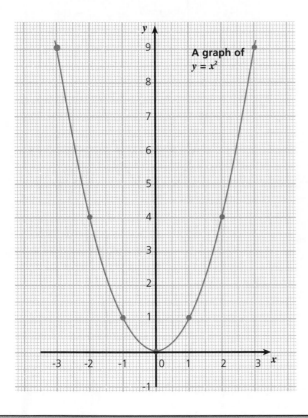

A graph of $y = x^2$

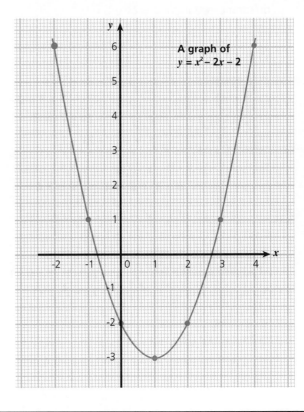

A graph of $y = x^2 - 2x - 2$

Graphs of Quadratic Functions

Solving Quadratic Equations Graphically

Approximate solutions to a quadratic equation can be found from the graph of the corresponding quadratic function.

The graph of $y = x^2 - 2x - 2$ (see page 47) can be used to solve the quadratic equation $x^2 - 2x - 2 = 0$.

Our quadratic equation is... $\boxed{x^2 - 2x - 2} = 0$

Our graph is... $y = \boxed{x^2 - 2x - 2}$

Since our quadratic equation corresponds to our quadratic function (i.e. $x^2 - 2x - 2$ is common to both), then approximate solutions are simply the x values where the graph crosses the line $y = 0$, i.e. the x-axis. The two approximate solutions to the equation $x^2 - 2x - 2 = 0$ are $x = -0.7$ and $x = 2.7$ (see graph opposite).

A graph of a quadratic function can also be used to solve a wide variety of quadratic equations. However, you will probably have to rearrange the quadratic equation so that it corresponds to the quadratic function before any solutions can be obtained.

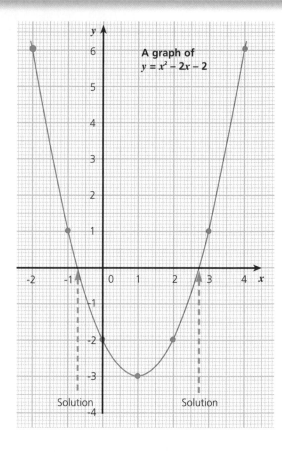

A graph of $y = x^2 - 2x - 2$

Solution   Solution

Examples

1 Use the graph of $y = x^2 - 2x - 2$ to solve the quadratic equation $x^2 - 2x - 5 = 0$.

Firstly, we need to rearrange the quadratic equation so that it corresponds to the quadratic function.

Our equation is... $x^2 - 2x - 5 = 0$

Add 3 to both sides $x^2 - 2x - 5 + 3 = 0 + 3$

Our equation now becomes... $\boxed{x^2 - 2x - 2} = 3$

Our graph is... $y = \boxed{x^2 - 2x - 2}$

The solutions are the x values where the graph crosses the line $y = 3$: $x = -1.4$ and $x = 3.4$

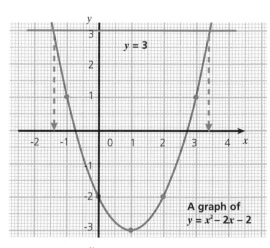

$y = 3$

A graph of $y = x^2 - 2x - 2$

2 Use the graph of $y = x^2 - 2x - 2$ to solve the quadratic equation $x^2 - 2x - 1 = 0$.

Our equation is... $x^2 - 2x - 1 = 0$

Subtract 1 from both sides $x^2 - 2x - 1 - 1 = 0 - 1$

Our equation now becomes... $\boxed{x^2 - 2x - 2} = -1$

Our graph is... $y = \boxed{x^2 - 2x - 2}$

This time the solutions are the x values where the graph crosses the line $y = -1$: $x = -0.4$ and $x = 2.4$

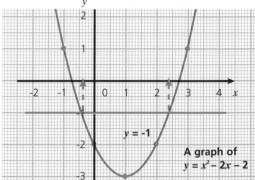

$y = -1$

A graph of $y = x^2 - 2x - 2$

Graphs of Other Functions

Graphs of Simple Cubic Functions

A cubic function is one that can be put in the form $y = ax^3 + bx^2 + cx + d$. Examples would include $y = x^3$, $y = x^3 + 1$, $y = 2x^3$. These functions always produce a curved graph with a double bend in it such as the one below. Again we need to plot a full range of points as this increases the accuracy of our curve, for example…

Draw the graph of $y = x^3$ for values of x between -3 and 3 (-3 ⩽ x ⩽ 3).

Table of results for $y = x^3$

x	-3	-2	-1	0	1	2	3
$y = x^3$	$(-3)^3=$ -27	$(-2)^3=$ -8	$(-1)^3=$ -1	$(0)^3=$ 0	$(1)^3=$ 1	$(2)^3=$ 8	$(3)^3=$ 27

Since we now have the coordinates of 7 points we can draw our graph. As before, your curve must be smooth and it must pass through all of the points plotted.

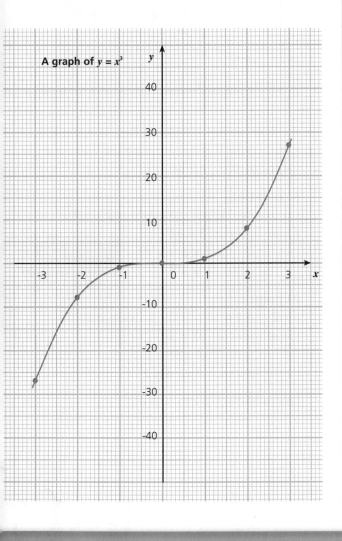

A graph of $y = x^3$

Graph of the Reciprocal Function

$$y = \frac{1}{x} \text{ with } x \neq 0$$

The reciprocal function $y = \frac{1}{x}$ with $x \neq 0$ gives us two separate curves.

For negative values of x…

x	-5	-4	-3	-2	-1	-0.5	-0.$\dot{3}$	-0.25	-0.2
$y = \frac{1}{x}$	-0.2	-0.25	-0.$\dot{3}$	-0.5	-1	-2	-3	-4	-5

For positive values of x…

x	0.2	0.25	0.$\dot{3}$	0.5	1	2	3	4	5
$y = \frac{1}{x}$	5	4	3	2	1	0.5	0.$\dot{3}$	0.25	0.2

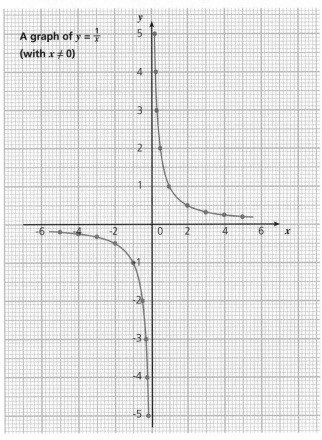

A graph of $y = \frac{1}{x}$ (with $x \neq 0$)

With the function $y = \frac{1}{x}$, for any point on either curve the x coordinate multiplied by the y coordinate always equals 1.

e.g. When $x = -2$, $y = -0.5$
to give us $x \times y = -2 \times -0.5 = 1$
When $x = 0.25$, $y = 4$
to give us $x \times y = 0.25 \times 4 = 1$

Graphs of Other Functions

Graphs of the Exponential Function
$y = k^x$

You need to be able to draw the graph of the exponential function $y = k^x$ for integer values of x and simple positive values of k.

Examples

① $y = k^x$ where $k > 1$, e.g. $y = 2^x$

x	0	1	2	3	4
$y = 2^x$	$(2)^0 =$ 1	$(2)^1 =$ 2	$(2)^2 =$ 4	$(2)^3 =$ 8	$(2)^4 =$ 16

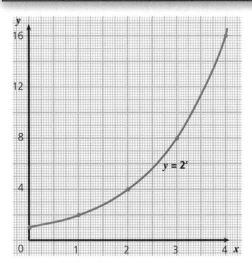

② $y = k^x$ where $0 < k < 1$, e.g. $y = (0.5)^x$

x	0	1	2	3	4
$y = (0.5)^x$	$(0.5)^0 =$ 1	$(0.5)^1 =$ 0.5	$(0.5)^2 =$ 0.25	$(0.5)^3 =$ 0.125	$(0.5)^4 =$ 0.0625

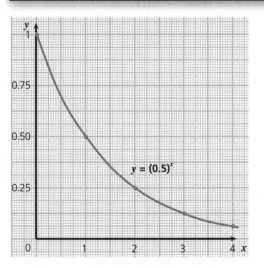

③ The graph below is known to fit the relationship $y = ab^x$. Use the graph to find the value of a and b and the relationship.

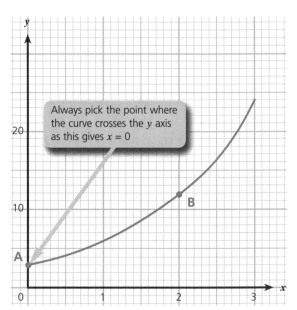

> Always pick the point where the curve crosses the y axis as this gives $x = 0$

This time we need to take values for x and y from our graph and then substitute them into the relationship, $y = ab^x$.

At point A:
$x = 0$ (curve crosses the y-axis) and $y = 3$
$y = ab^x$ gives us: $3 = ab^0$
$$3 = a \times 1$$

> Anything to the power of $0 = 1$

and so... $a = 3$

At point B:
$x = 2$ and $y = 12$ (we know that $a = 3$)
$y = ab^x$ gives us: $12 = 3b^2$
$$4 = b^2$$
and so... $b = \sqrt{4} = 2$

The relationship is: $y = 3 \times 2^x$

Graphs of Other Functions

xy

Graph of $y = \sin x$

If we plot the graph of $y = \sin x$ for values of x from **0°** to **360°** we get the following:

$x(°)$	0	30	60	90	120	150	180	210	240	270	300	330	360
$y = \sin x$	0	0.5	0.87	1	0.87	0.5	0	-0.5	-0.87	-1	-0.87	-0.5	0

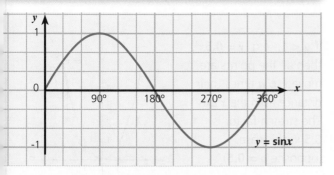

The graph is wave-like, where the maximum value of $\sin x$ is **1** when $x = $ **90°** and the minimum value of $\sin x$ is **-1** when $x = $ **270°**. When $x = $ **0°**, **180°** or **360°** the graph crosses the x-axis and $\sin x$ is equal to **0**.

The graph above is for values of x from **0°** to **360°**. It is also possible to extend beyond this range, i.e. values of x less than **0°** and greater than **360°**. The pattern or cycle repeats itself every **360°**, as shown in the graph below.

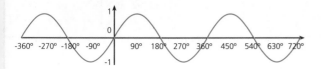

Graph of $y = \cos x$

If we plot the graph of $y = \cos x$ for values of x from **0°** to **360°** we get the following:

$x(°)$	0	30	60	90	120	150	180	210	240	270	300	330	360
$y = \cos x$	1	0.87	0.5	0	-0.5	-0.87	-1	-0.87	-0.5	0	0.5	0.87	1

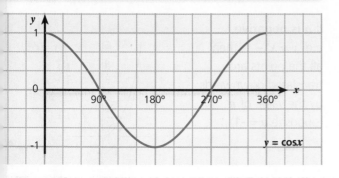

The graph is wave-like (same as the graph of $y = \sin x$, except that it has been shifted 90° to the left), where the maximum value of **cos x** is **1** when $x = $ **0°** or **360°** and the minimum value of **cos x** is **-1** when $x = $ **180°**. When $x = $ **90° or 270°** the graph crosses the x-axis and **cos x** is equal to **0**.

Also, as for the graph of $y = \sin x$, we can extend beyond **0°** and **360°**. The pattern again repeats itself every **360°**.

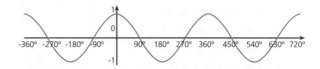

Graph of $y = \tan x$

If we plot the graph of $y = \tan x$ for values of x from **0°** to **360°** we get the following:

$x(°)$	0	30	60	90	120	150	180	210	240	270	300	330	360
$y = \tan x$	0	0.58	1.73	0	-1.73	-0.58	0	0.58	1.73	0	-1.73	-0.58	0

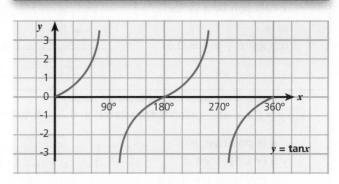

The graph is not wave-like like the **sin x** and **cos x** graphs. When $x = $ **90°** or **270°** then **tan x** is undefined. When $x = $ **0°**, **180°** or **360°** the graph crosses the x-axis and **tan x** is equal to **0**.

Also, we can extend beyond **0°** and **360°**. The pattern repeats itself every **180°**.

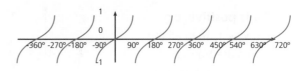

Transformation of Functions

Four Standard Transformations

If **y = an expression involving** *x* then we can say that *y* is a function of *x* or *y = f(x)*. You may well be asked to draw the graph of another function that is related to the graph of a function that has been already drawn for you.

Examples

1 *y = af(x)*… graph is **stretched** in the *y* direction

If *a* > 1, e.g. *y* = 2*x*², then all the points are stretched upwards in the *y* direction by a factor of *a* (opposite *a* = 2)

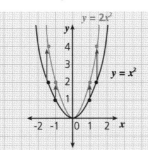

If *a* < 1, e.g. *y* = 0.5*x*², then all the points are moved to *a* times their distance from the *x* axis. The stretch factor is 0.5 in this case. (opposite *a* = 0.5)

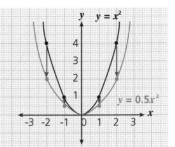

2 *y = f(ax)*… graph is **stretched** in the *x* direction

If *a* > 1, e.g. *y* = (2*x*)², then all the points are stretched inwards in the *x* direction by a factor of $\frac{1}{a}$
(opposite $\frac{1}{a} = \frac{1}{2} = 0.5$)

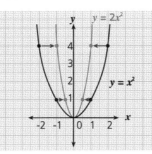

If *a* < 1, e.g. *y* = (0.5*x*)², then all the points are stretched outwards in the *x* direction by a factor of $\frac{1}{a}$
(opposite $\frac{1}{a} = \frac{1}{0.5} = 2$)

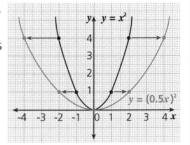

3 *y = f(x + a)*… graph is **translated** in the *x* direction

If *a* is positive, e.g. *y* = (*x* + 1)², then all the points are translated to the left by the value of *a* (opposite *a* = 1)

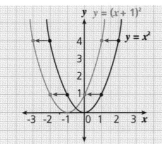

If *a* is negative, e.g. *y* = (*x* − 1)², then all the points are translated to the right by the value of *a* (opposite *a* = -1)

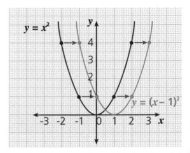

4 *y = f(x) + a*… graph is **translated** in the *y* direction

If *a* is positive, e.g. *y* = *x*² + 1, then all the points are translated upwards by the value of *a* (opposite *a* = 1)

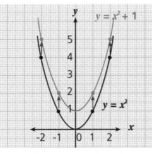

If *a* is negative, e.g. *y* = *x*² − 1, then all the points are translated downwards by the value of *a* (opposite *a* = -1)

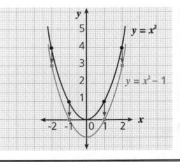

Conversion Graphs

These are used to convert values of one unit into another, e.g. pounds sterling (£) into dollars ($) or any other currency, miles into kilometres and so on.

Example

Draw a conversion graph for pounds sterling and dollars up to £300 if £1 = $1.60. From your graph convert…

a) £170 into dollars

b) $400 into pounds sterling.

Before we can draw our graph we need a table of values for pounds sterling and dollars.

Pounds Sterling (£)	Dollars ($)
100	(100 × 1.6 =) 160
200	(200 × 1.6 =) 320
300	(300 × 1.6 =) 480

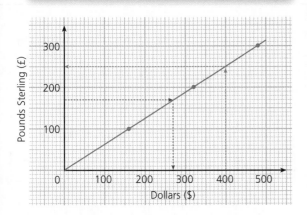

a) Go to £170 on the pounds sterling axis, draw a dotted line across (➡) to the graph and then down (⬇) to the dollars axis. **£170 = $270**

b) Go to $400 on the dollars axis, draw a dotted line up (⬆) to the graph and then across (⬅) to the pounds sterling axis. **$400 = £250**

Graphs that Describe Real Life Situations

Here are 6 examples (there are numerous others) where a graph can be used to show a real life situation.

All of these graphs require common sense in their interpretation as each one is very different.

Examples

1 Temperature at different times in the day

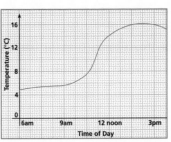

2 Weight of a man as he gets older

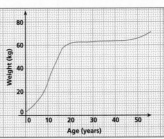

3 Value of a car as it gets older

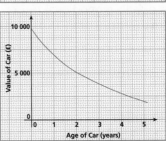

4 Pulse rate of a runner after the race is over

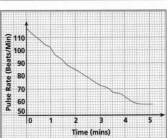

5 Height of a girl as she gets older

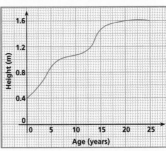

6 Temperature of a thermostatically controlled room over a period of time

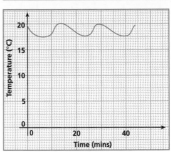

Direct and Inverse Proportion

Direct Proportion

Two quantities are in direct proportion if when we double (or treble) one of the quantities then the other quantity also doubles (or trebles). If two quantities, y and x, are in direct proportion, then a graph of values of y against values of x would be a straight line.

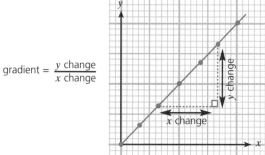

$$\text{gradient} = \frac{y \text{ change}}{x \text{ change}}$$

We can say that...

y is directly proportional to x or $y \propto x$ which means that $y = kx$ where k is a constant, i.e. a number that doesn't change and is given by the **gradient** of the graph.

It is also possible for $y \propto x^2$, $y \propto x^3$ and so on.

Example

The distance, d, travelled by an accelerating car that was initially stationary is directly proportional to the **square** of the time, t, of travel. The table below gives values of d and t. What is the relationship between d and t?

$t(s)$	0	1	2	3
$t^2(s)$	$(0^2=)\ 0$	$(1^2=)\ 1$	$(2^2=)\ 4$	$(3^2=)\ 9$
$d(m)$	0	3	12	27

Since $d \propto t^2$ or $d = kt^2$ we've added one row, t^2, to our table (shown in red). A graph of d against t^2 will give us a straight line.

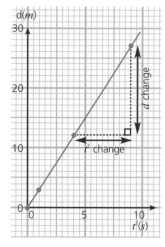

gradient $= k$

$$= \frac{d \text{ change}}{t^2 \text{ change}}$$

$$= \frac{(27-12)}{(9-4)}$$

$$= \frac{15}{5}$$

$$= 3$$

Relationship is...

$$d = 3t^2$$

Inverse Proportion

Two quantities are in inverse proportion if when we double (or treble) one of the quantities then the other quantity halves (or becomes a third). If two quantities y and x are in inverse proportion then a graph of values of y against values of $\frac{1}{x}$ would be a straight line.

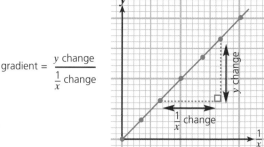

$$\text{gradient} = \frac{y \text{ change}}{\frac{1}{x} \text{ change}}$$

We can say that...

y is inversely proportional to x or $y \propto \frac{1}{x}$ which means that $y = \frac{k}{x}$ where k is a constant and is given by the gradient of the graph.

It is also possible for $y \propto \frac{1}{x^2}$, $y \propto \frac{1}{x^3}$ and so on.

Example

The density, d, of objects of fixed mass is inversely proportional to their volume, V. The table below gives values of d and V. What is the relationship between d and V?

$V(m^3)$	10	5	2	1
$\frac{1}{V}(m^3)$	$(\frac{1}{10}=)\ 0.1$	$(\frac{1}{5}=)\ 0.2$	$(\frac{1}{2}=)\ 0.5$	$(\frac{1}{1}=)\ 1$
$d(kg/m^3)$	1	2	5	10

Since $d \propto \frac{1}{V}$ or $d = \frac{k}{V}$ we've added one row, $\frac{1}{V}$, to our table (shown in red). A graph of d against $\frac{1}{V}$ will give us a straight line.

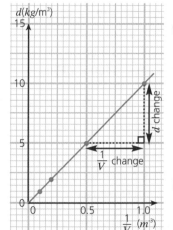

gradient $= k$

$$= \frac{d \text{ change}}{\frac{1}{V} \text{ change}}$$

$$= \frac{(10-5)}{(1-0.5)}$$

$$= \frac{5}{0.5}$$

$$= 10$$

Relationship is...

$$d = \frac{10}{V}$$

Angles

Acute, Right, Obtuse and Reflex Angles

All angles are measured in **degrees** (°). A protractor can be used to measure the size of an angle.

An angle less than 90° is called an **acute angle**.

An angle equal to 90° is called a **right angle**.

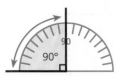
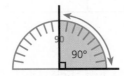

An angle greater than 90° but less than 180° is called an **obtuse angle**.

An angle greater than 180° is called a **reflex angle**.

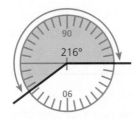

Angles on a Straight Line

Angles on a straight line add up to 180° (also known as Adjacent Angles).

$a = 120°$
$b = 60°$ $a + b = 180°$

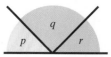

$p = 45°$
$q = 90°$ $p + q + r = 180°$
$r = 45°$

Angles at a Point

Angles at a point add up to 360°.

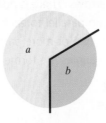

$a = 240°$
$b = 120°$ $a + b = 360°$

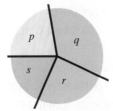

$p = 80°$
$q = 125°$
$r = 90°$ $p + q + r + s = 360°$
$s = 65°$

Vertically opposite angles are equal.

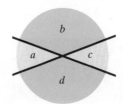

$a = 40°$
$c = 40°$ } Vertically opposite
$b = 140°$
$d = 140°$ } Vertically opposite

Examples

① Work out the angles $a + b$

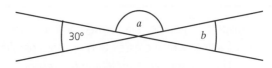

$a = 180° - 30° = 150°$
(Angles on a straight line add up to 180°)
$b = 30°$ (Vertically opposite angles are equal)

② Work out the angle c

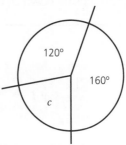

$c = 360° - (120° + 160°)$
$c = 360° - 280° = 80°$
(Angles at a point add up to 360°)

Angles

Parallel Lines

Parallel lines run in exactly the same direction and never meet. Parallel lines are shown by arrows. There is no limit to the number of lines that may run parallel to each other. When a straight line crosses two or more parallel lines, corresponding and alternate angles are formed.

Alternate Angles and Corresponding Angles

- Alternate angles are formed on opposite (alternate) sides of a line that crosses two or more parallel lines.
- Alternate angles are always equal in size.
- Alternate angles can be easily spotted because they form a letter Z (although sometimes it may be reversed Σ).

Example

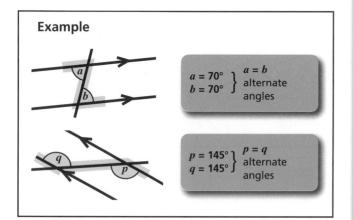

$a = 70°$
$b = 70°$ } $a = b$ alternate angles

$p = 145°$
$q = 145°$ } $p = q$ alternate angles

- Corresponding angles are formed on the same side of a line, which crosses two or more parallel lines. They all appear in matching (corresponding) positions above or below the parallel lines.
- Corresponding angles are always equal in size.
- Corresponding angles can be easily spotted because they form a letter F (although sometimes it may be reversed, ⅂, or upside down ⅃, Ⅎ).

Example

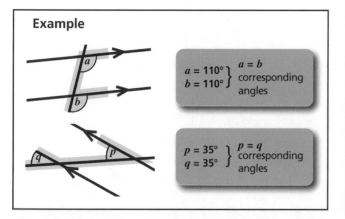

$a = 110°$
$b = 110°$ } $a = b$ corresponding angles

$p = 35°$
$q = 35°$ } $p = q$ corresponding angles

Angle Proofs

The diagram shows triangle ABC with the side AC extended to D and CE drawn parallel to AB.

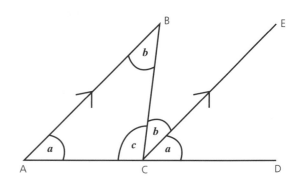

- The two angles labelled **a** are equal as they are corresponding angles.
- The two angles labelled **b** are equal as they are alternate angles.
- At point C angles **a**, **b** and **c** lie on the straight line ACD, so **a + b + c = 180°**

This proves that the sum of the angles of a triangle is 180°

- Angle BCD is an exterior angle of the triangle. **Angle BCD = a + b**
- The interior angles opposite to C are **a** and **b**

This proves that the exterior angle of a triangle is equal to the sum of the two interior opposite angles.

Example
Calculate the value of x.

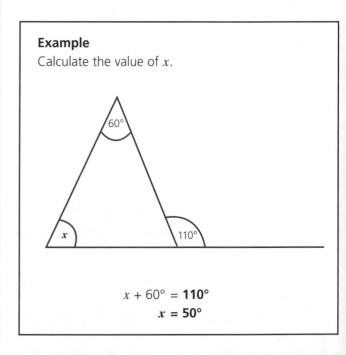

$$x + 60° = 110°$$
$$x = 50°$$

Angles of Polygons

Interior Angles of a Polygon

The diagram shows a pentagon ABCDE divided into three triangles.

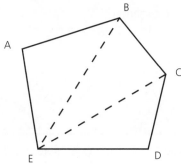

The angles inside each triangle add up to 180° and these combine to make the interior angles of the pentagon.

So, the sum of the interior angles of a pentagon is
3 × 180° = 540°.

A hexagon may be divided into four triangles in the same way.

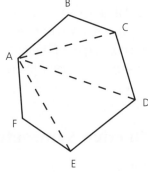

So, the sum of the interior angles of a hexagon is
4 × 180° = 720°.

In general, a polygon with n sides may be divided into $(n - 2)$ triangles.

Therefore, the sum of the interior angles of an n-sided polygon is **$(n - 2) \times 180°$**.

Example

The sum of the interior angles of a polygon is 3240°. How many sides does it have?

$$(n - 2) \times 180 = 3240$$
$$n - 2 = \frac{3240}{180}$$
$$= 18$$
$$n = 20$$

The polygon has 20 sides.

Interior and Exterior Angles

An exterior angle is formed by extending one side of a polygon. In the diagram, the side DE is extended to F.

Angle **AED** is an interior angle.
Angle **AEF** is an exterior angle.

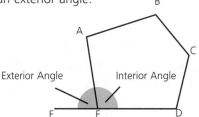

The interior and exterior angles at a vertex always make a straight line and always add up to 180°.

The sum of all of the exterior angles of a polygon is always 360°.

Regular Polygons

Regular polygons have…

- all sides of the same length
- all interior angles of the same size
- all exterior angles of the same size

Example

Calculate the size of **a)** each exterior, and **b)** each interior angle for a regular hexagon (6 sides).

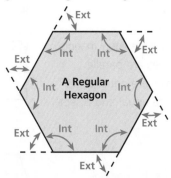

A regular hexagon has 6 equal interior angles and 6 equal exterior angles.

a) The exterior angles of a hexagon add up to 360°

Each exterior angle = $\frac{360°}{6}$ = 60°

b) The interior angle + the exterior angle add up to 180°

Each interior angle = 180° − exterior angle
= 180° − 60°
= **120°**

Quadrilaterals and Symmetry

Types of Quadrilateral

A quadrilateral is a 4-sided, two-dimensional shape, which has interior angles that add up to 360°.

Square
- All the sides are equal in length
- Opposite sides are parallel
- All the angles are equal to 90°
- Diagonals are equal and bisect each other at right-angles.
- Diagonals also bisect each of the interior angles.

Parallelogram
- Opposite sides are equal in length
- Opposite sides are parallel
- Opposite angles are equal in size
- Diagonals bisect each other.

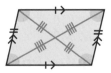

Rhombus
- All the sides are equal in length
- Opposite sides are parallel
- Opposite angles are equal in size
- Diagonals bisect each other at right-angles
- Diagonals also bisect the interior angles.

Rectangle
- Opposite sides are equal in length
- Opposite sides are parallel
- All the angles are equal to 90°
- Diagonals are equal and bisect each other.

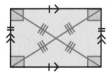

Trapezium
- One pair of sides parallel

Kite
- 2 pairs of equal adjacent sides
- 1 pair of opposite equal angles
- Diagonals cross at right-angles and one bisects the other.

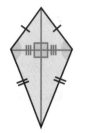

> Bisect means to divide into two equal parts.

The Interior Angles of a Quadrilateral

In this quadrilateral…

$a = 63°$, $b = 106°$, $c = 145°$, $d = 46°$

If we add these together…

$63° + 106° + 145° + 46° = 360°$

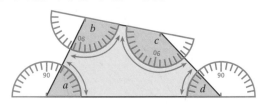

The sum of four angles in a quadrilateral willl always equal 360° and can be proved by dividing the quadrilateral into 2 triangles:

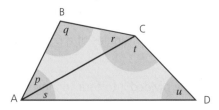

$p + q + r = 180°$ (Interior angles of a triangle)
$s + t + u = 180°$ (Interior angles of a triangle)

The sum of the interior angles of the quadrilateral is
$(p + s) + q + (r + t) + u$ which is therefore equal to
$(p + q + r) + (s + t + u)$
i.e. $180° + 180° = 360°$

Line or Reflective Symmetry

One Line of Symmetry

A two-dimensional shape has a **line of symmetry** if it can be 'cut in half' so that one half of the shape is an exact mirror image of the other half.

The shapes below have 1 line of symmetry. These shapes can be 'cut in half' only once, and one half of the shape is congruent to the other half.

> The left-hand side of the dotted line is an exact mirror image of the right-hand side and vice-versa.

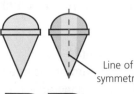

Line of symmetry

> The top side of the dotted line is an exact mirror image of the bottom side and vice-versa

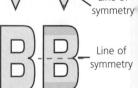

Line of symmetry

It is also possible for shapes to have more than 1 line of symmetry. The shapes on p59 can be 'cut in half' more than once. A simple way to find lines of symmetry is to use tracing paper.

Symbol

Symmetry

Two Lines of Symmetry

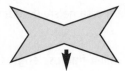

Draw in where you think the line of symmetry is and trace one side of your shape carefully on the tracing paper.

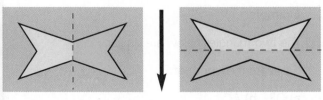

Flip the tracing paper over about the line of symmetry. If your line of symmetry is correct you should get an exact mirror image.

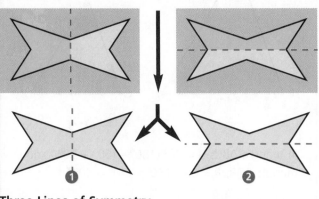

Three Lines of Symmetry

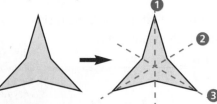

Four Lines of Symmetry

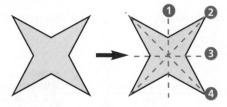

Some shapes, especially regular polygons, can have even more lines of symmetry. However, there are shapes that have **no line of symmetry**. The shapes below cannot be 'cut in half' to give exact mirror images.

Rotational Symmetry

A two-dimensional shape has **rotational symmetry** if it can be 'rotated about a point', called the Centre of Rotation, to a different position where it looks the same as it did to begin with. The Order of Rotational Symmetry is equal to the number of times a shape fits onto itself in one 360° turn.

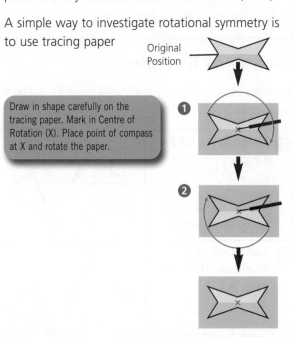

Example

The following shape has rotational symmetry of **order 2**. This shape looks the same as its original position every time it is rotated half a turn (180°).

A simple way to investigate rotational symmetry is to use tracing paper

Draw in shape carefully on the tracing paper. Mark in Centre of Rotation (X). Place point of compass at X and rotate the paper.

The following shape has rotational symmetry of order 3:

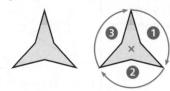

Some shapes, especially regular polygons, can have rotational symmetry of even higher orders. However, there are shapes that have **rotational symmetry of order 1 (no rotational symmetry)**. These shapes only look the same as their original position when they have been rotated one complete turn (360°).

Congruence and Similiarity

Congruent Figures

Congruent figures have the same shape and size.

Example

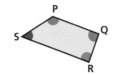

Figure ABCD and figure PQRS are congruent because $\hat{A} = \hat{P}$, $\hat{B} = \hat{Q}$, $\hat{C} = \hat{R}$ and $\hat{D} = \hat{S}$.

Two congruent figures have angles the same size and have sides of the same length. So AB = PQ, BC = QR, CD = RS and DA = SP.

Congruent Triangles

Two triangles are congruent if they satisfy the following conditions:

①	**Three Sides, SSS** AB = PQ BC = QR AC = PR ∴ ABC and PQR are congruent triangles.	
②	**Two Sides and Included Angle, SAS** AB = PQ AC = PR $\hat{A} = \hat{P}$ ∴ ABC and PQR are congruent triangles.	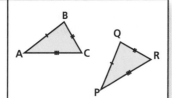
③	**Two Angles and One Corresponding Side, ASA** AB = PQ $\hat{A} = \hat{P}$ $\hat{B} = \hat{Q}$ ∴ ABC and PQR are congruent triangles.	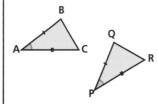 Note: In our diagram we've used AB = PQ. However we could have used BC = QR or AC = PR. The two triangles are still congruent.
④	**Right Angle, Hypotenuse and One Other Side, RHS** AB = PQ BC = QR $\hat{C} = \hat{R}$ = 90° ∴ ABC and PQR are congruent triangles.	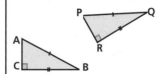 Note: In our diagram we've used BC = QR. However we could have used AC = PR. The two triangles would still be congruent.

Similar Figures

Similar figures have the same shape but may be different in size.

When comparing similar figures, lengths of corresponding sides are in the same ratio.

Example

The two triangles below are similar.

Calculate the length of…

a) QR   **b)** AC

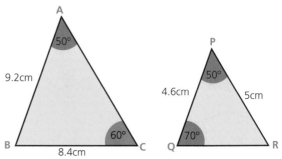

In triangle ABC, $\hat{B}$ = 70° (180° − (60° + 50°)) and in triangle PQR, $\hat{R}$ = 60° (180° − (70° + 50°))

And so $\hat{A} = \hat{P}$, $\hat{B} = \hat{Q}$, $\hat{C} = \hat{R}$

This means that triangle ABC is similar to triangle PQR which means that…

$$\frac{AB}{PQ} = \frac{BC}{QR} = \frac{AC}{PR}$$

> Don't assume that the shapes (in this case triangles) are always lettered in alphabetical order

$$\frac{9.2cm}{4.6cm} = \frac{8.4cm}{QR} = \frac{AC}{5cm}$$

We can now calculate the unknown lengths…

a) $\frac{9.2cm}{4.6cm} = \frac{8.4cm}{QR}$

$QR = \frac{8.4cm \times 4.6cm}{9.2cm}$

> Rearranged to get QR on its own

$QR = \textbf{4.2cm}$

b) $\frac{9.2cm}{4.6cm} = \frac{AC}{5cm}$

$AC = \frac{9.2cm \times 5cm}{4.6cm}$

> Rearranged to get AC on its own

$AC = \textbf{10cm}$

Pythagoras

Pythagoras' theorem states that in any right-angled triangle the square on the hypotenuse is equal to the sum of the squares on the other two sides.

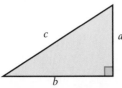

The theorem may be written in algebra as $c^2 = a^2 + b^2$. You can rearrange this to calculate one of the shorter sides, e.g. $a^2 = c^2 - b^2$.

Examples

1 Calculate the length of c in the following right-angled triangle.

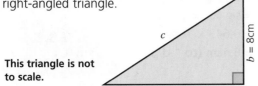

This triangle is not to scale.

$a = 6\text{cm}$, $b = 8\text{cm}$

Using Pythagoras' Theorem
$c^2 = a^2 + b^2$
$c^2 = 6^2 + 8^2$
$c^2 = 36 + 64$
$c^2 = 100$

To get c we need to take the square root.
$c = \sqrt{100}$
$c = \mathbf{10\text{cm}}$ (remember the units)

2 Calculate the height of the isosceles triangle (to 3 s.f.)

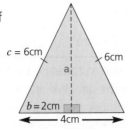

$c = 6\text{cm}$, 6cm, a, $b = 2\text{cm}$, 4cm

First we must divide the triangle into two right-angled triangles (as shown by the dotted line) in order to use Pythagoras' theorem and label the one we are going to work with (in red).
$a^2 = c^2 - b^2$
$a^2 = 6^2 - 2^2$
$a^2 = 36 - 4$
$a^2 = 32$
To get a we need to take the square root
$a = \sqrt{32} = \mathbf{5.66\text{cm}}$

Pythagoras' Theorem in 3-D

Pythagoras' Theorem may be adapted to work in three dimensions. The diagram shows a cuboid with edges of length a, b and c.

The length of one diagonal is d where $d^2 = e^2 + c^2$

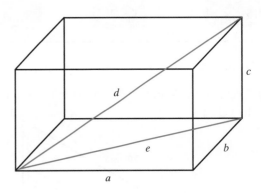

But $e^2 = a^2 + b^2$ so, $d^2 = a^2 + b^2 + c^2$

Example

Calculate the length of the red diagonal shown, to 1 d.p.

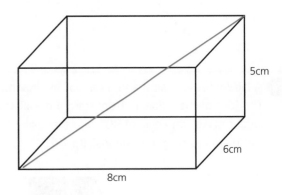

5cm, 6cm, 8cm

Using $d^2 = a^2 + b^2 + c^2$
$d^2 = 8^2 + 6^2 + 5^2$
$d^2 = 125$
$d = \sqrt{125} = 11.18...$

The length of the diagonal is **11.2 cm to 1 d.p**

Trigonometry

Calculating the Length of an Unknown Side

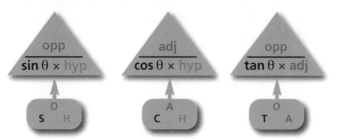

In this form, the three triganometrical ratios – sine, cosine and tangent – can be used to calculate unknown sides and angles in **right-angled triangles**. The formula triangles make it easy to rearrange each ratio as required, e.g.

$$\sin \theta = \frac{opp}{hyp}$$

$$opp = \sin \theta \times hyp$$

$$hyp = \frac{opp}{\sin \theta}$$

Examples

1 Calculate the length of BC in the following triangle (to 1 d.p.).

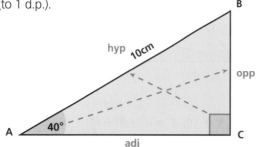

We want to calculate the length of the **opposite** side and we are given the **hypotenuse**, so we need to use the trigonometrical ratio for **sin** (S O H). We can now use the formula triangle to rearrange the sin ratio:

$opp = \sin \theta \times hyp$

BC $= \sin 40° \times 10$cm

BC $= 0.643 \times 10$cm

BC $= 6.4$cm (to 1 d.p.)

---

2 Calculate the length of AB in the following triangle

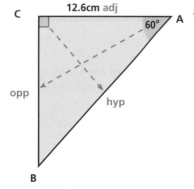

We want to calculate the length of the **hypotenuse** and we are given the **adjacent**, so we need to use the trigonometrical ratio for **cos** (C A H). We can now use the formula triangle to rearrange the cos ratio:

$$hyp = \frac{adj}{\cos \theta}$$

$$AB = \frac{12.6cm}{\cos 60°}$$

$$AB = \frac{12.6}{0.5}$$

AB = 25.2cm

---

3 A ladder leans against a vertical wall as shown below. The foot of the ladder is 1.6m from the wall and the ladder makes an angle of 30° with the wall. Calculate the height of the wall (to 1 d.p.).

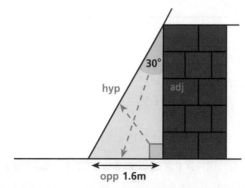

We want to calculate the height of the wall – the **adjacent** side. We are given the **opposite** side, so we need to use the trigonometrical ratio for **tan** (T O A). We can now use the formula triangle to rearrange the tan ratio:

$$adj = \frac{opp}{\tan \theta}$$

$$adj = \frac{1.6m}{\tan 30°}$$

$$adj = \frac{1.6}{0.577}$$

height of wall = 2.8m (to 1 d.p.)

Trigonometry

Calculating the Size of an Unknown Angle

Example

Calculate the size of angle BAC in the following triangle.

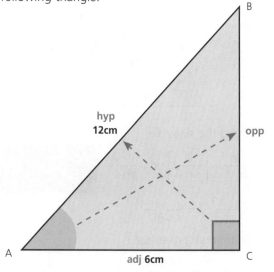

Since we are given the adjacent and hypotenuse, we need to use the trigonomic ratio for cos (C A H).

$$\cos \theta = \frac{adj}{hyp}$$

There is no need to use a formula triangle to calculate the size of an unknown angle. However you still need to remember 'SOH CAH TOA'

$$\cos B\hat{A}C = \frac{6cm}{12cm}$$

$$\cos B\hat{A}C = 0.5$$

$$B\hat{A}C = \cos^{-1}(0.5)$$

To calculate B$\hat{A}$C we now have to use the INVERSE cos button on our calculator, i.e. the cos^{-1} button, to get the answer

$$\mathbf{B\hat{A}C = 60°}$$

Angles of Elevation and Depression

Angles of elevation and depression are both measured from the horizontal direction either upwards or downwards.

A child looking up at an adult…

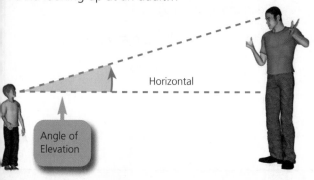

An adult looking down at a child…

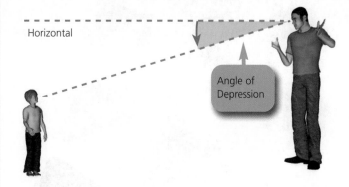

These two angles will always be equal.

Example

The tree in the diagram below is 9m high.

Calculate the angle of elevation to the top of the tree from a point on the ground 20m from the foot of the tree (to 1 d.p.).

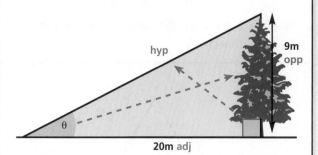

We want to calculate the angle of elevation (θ) and we are given the opposite and adjacent, so we need to use the trigonomic ratio for tan (T O A).

$$\tan \theta = \frac{opp}{adj}$$

$$\tan \theta = \frac{9m}{20m}$$

To calculate the angle of elevation θ, we now have to use the inverse tan button on our calculator, i.e. the tan^{-1} button to get the answer

$$\tan \theta = 0.45$$

$$\theta = \tan^{-1}(0.45)$$

Angle of Elevation = 24.2° (to 1 d.p.)

Trigonometry

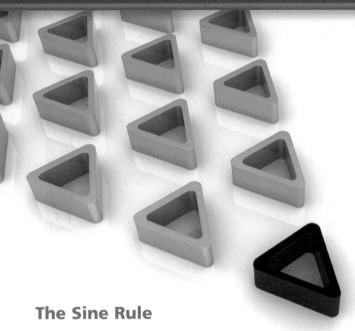

The Sine Rule

The sine rule can be used in any triangle to calculate the length of an unknown side or the size of an unknown angle:

$$\frac{a}{\sin A} = \frac{b}{\sin B} = \frac{c}{\sin C}$$

where a, b and c are the sides opposite angles A, B and C respectively.

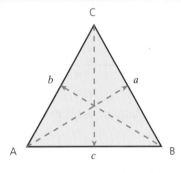

You can only use **two** parts of the sine rule at any one time:

$$\frac{a}{\sin A} = \frac{b}{\sin B} \quad \text{or} \quad \frac{a}{\sin A} = \frac{c}{\sin C} \quad \text{or} \quad \frac{b}{\sin B} = \frac{c}{\sin C}$$

The sine rule can be used to calculate…

- the length of an unknown side, if we are given the length of one other side and the size of two angles.
- the size of an unknown angle, if we are given the length of two sides and the size of an angle opposite one of these sides.

Note: The sine rule can be used to solve problems in 2-D or 3-D. It can also be used with right-angled triangles, but it is better to use the three trigonometry ratios – sin, cos and tan – as they are a lot easier.

Examples

1 Calculate the length of AB in the following triangle (to 2 d.p.).

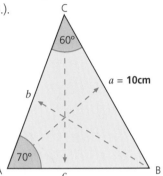

Using the sine rule…

$$\frac{a}{\sin A} = \left[\frac{b}{\sin B}\right] \text{or} = \frac{c}{\sin C}$$

> Since b and sin B play no part in the question, ignore them.

$$\therefore \frac{10}{\sin 70°} = \frac{c}{\sin 60°}$$

Rearranging gives us…

$$c = \frac{10 \times \sin 60°}{\sin 70°}$$

$$c = 9.22\text{cm}$$

$\therefore$ Length of AB = **9.22cm**

2 Calculate angle ABC in the following triangle (to 1 d.p.).

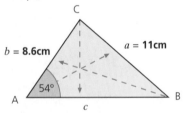

Using the sine rule…

$$\frac{a}{\sin A} = \frac{b}{\sin B} \text{ or } = \left[\frac{c}{\sin C}\right]$$

> Since c and sin C play no part in the question, ignore them.

$$\therefore \frac{11}{\sin 54°} = \frac{8.6\text{cm}}{\sin B}$$

Rearranging gives us…

$$\sin B = \frac{8.6 \times \sin 54°}{11} = 0.6325$$

$$\hat{B} = \sin^{-1}(0.6325) = 39.23°$$

Size of $A\hat{B}C$ = **39.2°**

Trigonometry

The Cosine Rule

The cosine rule, like the sine rule, can be used in any triangle to calculate the length of an unknown side or the size of an unknown angle:

$$a^2 = b^2 + c^2 - 2bc \cos A$$

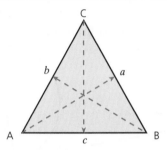

We rearrange the formula to find the size of an unknown angle:

$$\cos A = \frac{b^2 + c^2 - a^2}{2bc}$$

If we wanted to use the cosine rule to find the length of b or c then it becomes:

$$b^2 = a^2 + c^2 - 2ac \cos B$$
$$c^2 = a^2 + b^2 - 2ab \cos C$$

Also for angles B and C it becomes:

$$\cos B = \frac{a^2 + c^2 - b^2}{2ac}$$

$$\cos C = \frac{a^2 + b^2 - c^2}{2ab}$$

The cosine rule (compare to the sine rule) can be used to calculate…

- the length of an unknown side if we are given the length of two sides and the size of their included angle.
- the size of an unknown angle if we are given the length of all three sides

N.B. Like the sine rule, the cosine rule can be used to solve problems in 2D or 3D. Also it can be used with right-angled triangles, but you should always use the three trigonometry ratios – sin, cos and tan – as they are a lot easier.

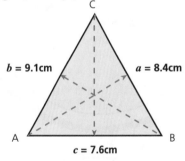

Examples

1 Calculate the length of BC in the following triangle (to 2 d.p.).

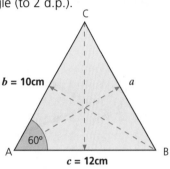

Using the cosine rule:
$$\begin{aligned}
a^2 &= b^2 + c^2 - 2bc \cos A \\
&= 10^2 + 12^2 - (2 \times 10 \times 12 \times \cos 60°) \\
&= 100 + 144 - (2 \times 10 \times 12 \times 0.5) \\
&= 100 + 144 - 120 \\
&= 124
\end{aligned}$$
$$a = \sqrt{124} = 11.14 \text{cm}$$
∴ Length of **BC = 11.14cm**

It would be impossible for you to calculate the length of BC using the sine rule – try it!

2 Calculate the size of $\hat{BAC}$ in the following triangle (to 2 d.p.).

Using the cosine rule (rearranged):

$$\cos A = \frac{b^2 + c^2 - a^2}{2bc}$$

$$= \frac{9.1^2 + 7.6^2 - 8.4^2}{2 \times 9.1 \times 7.6}$$

$$= \frac{82.81 + 57.76 - 70.56}{138.32}$$

$$\cos A = 0.5061$$
$$\hat{A} = \cos^{-1}(0.5061) = 59.60°$$
∴ size of $\hat{BAC}$ = **59.60°**

Again it would be impossible for you to calculate the size of $\hat{BAC}$ using the sine rule – try it!

Circles

Circles

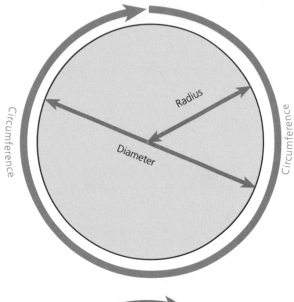

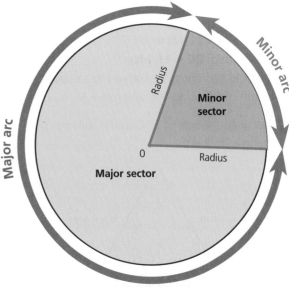

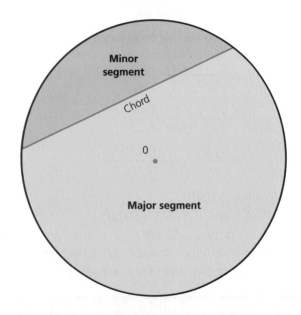

Chords, Tangents and Radii

There are several useful properties relating to chords and tangents of circles. You need to understand the first two of these on this page, but you must understand and be able to explain the third.

1 Tangent and Radius

A tangent is a straight line which touches the circumference of a circle. A tangent at any point on a circle is perpendicular to the radius at that point.

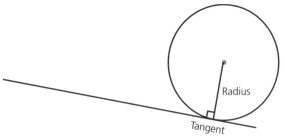

2 Two External Tangents

Tangents from an external point are equal in length, **PQ = PR**. This produces a symmetrical situation in which there are two congruent, right-angled triangles, PQO and PRO.

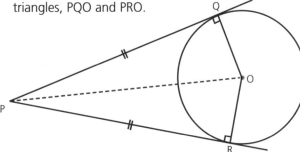

3 Perpendicular to a Chord

A chord is a straight line joining two points on the circumference, which does not pass through the centre of the circle.

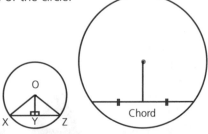

The perpendicular from the centre of a circle to a chord bisects the chord. The reason for this is as follows:

OX = OZ (both radii)
OY = OY (same line)
angle XYO = angle ZYO (90°)

Therefore, the triangles **XOY** and **ZOY** are congruent (RHS), which means that **XY = ZY**

Circles

Circles and Angles

The following two pages have five more facts relating to circles and angles. You need to know them and their proofs.

Circles and Angles	Proofs
1 Angles subtended by an arc The angle at the centre of a circle, subtended by an arc, is twice the angle subtended at any point on the circumference by the same arc. (**Note:** The word subtended simply means to be produced by drawing straight lines.) 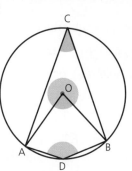	Triangle ACD is isosceles (OC and OA are equal) Angle OAC = x (angles in an isosceles triangle) Angle AOD = $2x$ (exterior angle of triangle AOC) Similarly, angle BOD = $2y$ 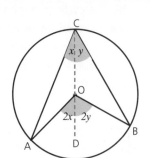
Angle AOB = 2 × Angle ACB Reflex Angle AOB = 2 × Angle ADB	Angle AOB = $2x + 2y = 2(x + y)$ **= 2 × Angle AĈB**
2 Angles subtended in the same segment Angles subtended in the same segment are all equal. Here the angles subtended by the chord AB in the major segment are equal. The angles subtended by the chord AB in the minor segment are also equal. 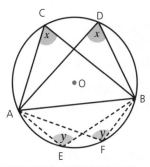	$\hat{AOB} = 2 \times \hat{ACB}$ (Angles subtended by an arc – see **1**) $\hat{AOB} = 2 \times \hat{ADB}$ (Angles subtended by an arc – see **1**) $\therefore \hat{ACB} = \hat{ADB}$ 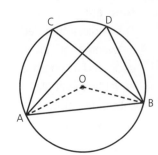
Angle ACB = Angle ADB Angle AEB = Angle AFB	
3 Angles subtended by a semicircle The angles subtended by a semicircle are always 90°. 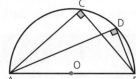	Let angle CAO = x and so angle ACO = x (isosceles triangle). 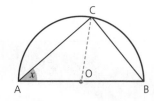 Angle BOC = $2x$ (exterior angle of triangle AOC) $\therefore \hat{BCO} = \frac{180° - \hat{BOC}}{2} = \frac{180° - 2x}{2} = 90° - x$ (Isosceles triangle) $\hat{ACB} = \hat{ACO} + \hat{BCO} = x + (90° - x) = \mathbf{90°}$
Angle ACB = Angle ADB = 90°	

Circles

Circles and Angles	Proofs
④ Opposite angles of a cyclic quadrilateral Opposite angles of a cyclic quadrilateral add up to 180°. A cyclic quadrilateral is a quadrilateral whose vertices (corners) all lie on the circumference of the same circle. 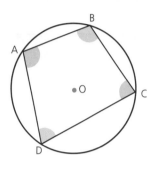	Let $B\hat{O}D = 2x$ $\therefore B\hat{A}D = \dfrac{B\hat{O}D}{2} = \dfrac{2x}{2} = x$ (Angles subtended by an arc) Reflex $B\hat{O}D = 360° - 2x$ (Angles at a point) $\therefore BCD = \dfrac{\text{Reflex } B\hat{O}D}{2} = \dfrac{360° - 2x}{2}$ $\qquad = 180° - x$ (Angles subtended by an arc) $B\hat{A}D + B\hat{C}D = x + (180° - x) = 180°$ **Consequently $A\hat{B}C + A\hat{D}C = 180°$** (Angles of a quadrilateral = 360°)

Angle BAD + Angle BCD = 180°
Angle ABC + Angle ADC = 180°

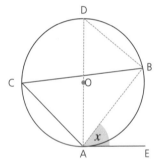

⑤ Alternate segment theorem The angle subtended between a tangent to a circle and its chord is equal to the angle subtended in the alternate segment. 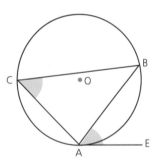	Let angle BAE = x and triangle ABD have AD as diameter. Angle ABD = 90° (angle in a semicircle) Angle BAD = 90° − x (angle between tangent and radius = 90°). Angle BAD + Angle ABD = 90° − x + 90° = 180° − x Angle ADB = x (angles in a triangle) **Angle ACB = Angle ADB** (angles subtended in the same segment) **Angle ACB = Angle BAE**

Angle ACB = Angle BAE

Nets, Plans and Elevations

Plans and Elevations

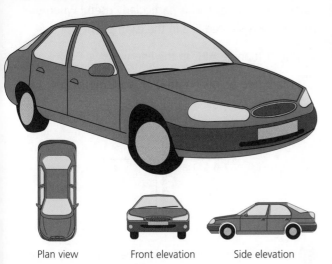

| Plan view | Front elevation | Side elevation |

This is a picture of a car (a three-dimensional view of a solid). It is possible for us to have three different views of the car:

- plan view where we look down on the car from above.
- front elevation where we look at the car from the front.
- side elevation where we look at the car from the side.

Examples

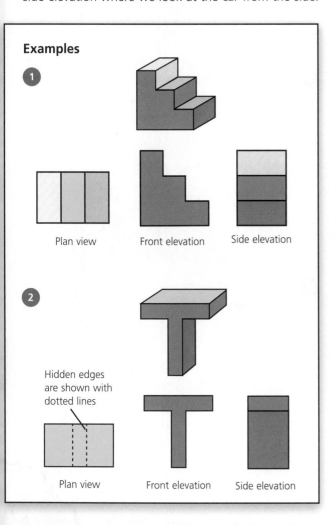

1

| Plan view | Front elevation | Side elevation |

2

Hidden edges are shown with dotted lines

| Plan view | Front elevation | Side elevation |

Nets for Solids

A net is a two-dimensional shape that can be folded to completely cover the outside of a solid.

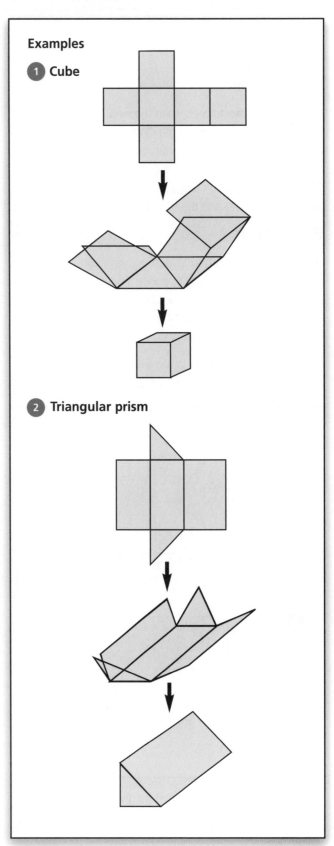

Examples

1 Cube

2 Triangular prism

Transformations

Types of Transformation

A **transformation** acts on every point of a shape and may change its size, position and orientation. You need to know about the following types of transformation:

- **reflection**
- **rotation**
- **translation**
- **enlargement.**

If a point A is transformed, then the new point is usually labelled A'. An inverted comma (') after the label is used to denote a point on a transformed image. The original point A is called the **object** and A' is called the **image**. Similarly, when a transformation is applied to a shape, the original shape is the object and the transformed shape is the image.

Reflection

A **mirror line** is needed to define a reflection. The image of every point lies on the opposite side of the mirror line to the object and is the same distance from the mirror line. A line drawn from the object to the image will cross the mirror line at right-angles.

To reflect a triangle ABC in a mirror line, find the image of each vertex and join them up to make triangle A'B'C'.

Examples

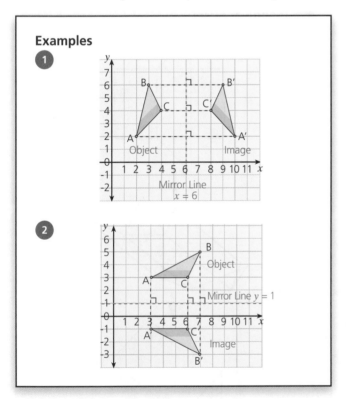

A mirror line is often described by giving its equation.

When a shape is reflected the image is congruent to the object, which means corresponding lengths and angles

are unchanged (see page 60). Tracing paper may be used to reflect a shape. This is particularly useful when the mirror line is slanted like in the example below.

To reflect triangle ABC in the line $y = x$...

1 Mark two points (● and ●) on your mirror line.

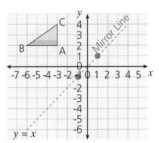

2 On the tracing paper, draw in the mirror line, mark points and object carefully. Then flip the tracing paper over (don't just rotate it!)...

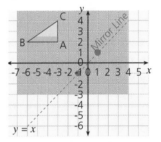

3 ... making sure that you line up the mirror line and marked points with the original. Mark the position of the image through the tracing paper.

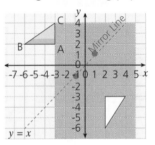

4 Remove the tracing paper. Draw in image and label.

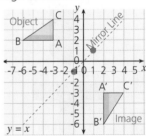

Note that when a point is reflected in the line $y = x$, the coordinates of the point are reversed. If A is the point (x, y) then A' is the point (y, x).

Rotation

A rotation turns a shape through a clockwise or anti-clockwise angle about a fixed point known as the Centre of Rotation. All lines in the shape rotate through the same angle. Rotation (just like reflection) changes the orientation and position of the shape, but everything else stays the same, i.e. length and angle. The object and image are congruent shapes (see page 60). To describe a rotation, you must specify the following three things:

- The direction of turn (clockwise / anti-clockwise)
- The centre of rotation
- The angle turned

Examples

Rotation of 90° clockwise about the origin (0,0)

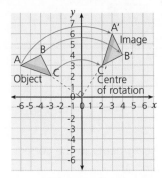

Rotation of 180° about the origin (0,0)

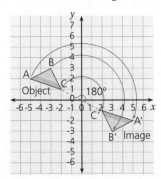

Rotation of 270° clockwise about the origin (0,0) (is the same as a rotation of 90° anti-clockwise)

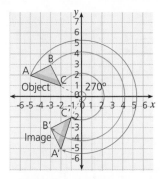

Difficult rotations can be completed more easily if you use tracing paper. If we wanted to rotate triangle ABC 90° clockwise about the centre (-1,1)…

1 On the tracing paper, draw in axes and object carefully.

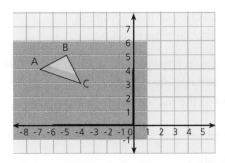

2 Place point of compass on centre of rotation (-1,1) and rotate paper clockwise.

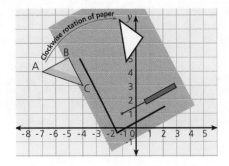

3 After 90° rotation, mark in position of image.

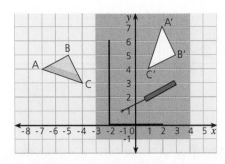

4 Remove the tracing paper. Draw in image and label.

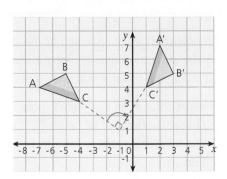

Transformations

Translation

A translation alters the position of a shape by moving every point of it by the same distance in the same direction. To describe a translation, you must specify the following two things:

- The direction of the movement
- The distance moved

This can be summarised using a **translation vector**. Positive and negative numbers are used to indicate the direction of the movement.

Examples

ABC has been translated to A''B''C'' by moving 11 squares to the left and then 4 squares down. This translation is written as a vector $\begin{pmatrix} -11 \\ -4 \end{pmatrix}$

ABC has been translated to A'B'C' by moving 7 squares to the right and then 2 squares up. This translation is written as a vector $\begin{pmatrix} 7 \\ 2 \end{pmatrix}$

ABC has been translated to A'''B'''C''' by moving 6 squares to the right and then 7 squares down. This translation is written as a vector $\begin{pmatrix} 6 \\ -7 \end{pmatrix}$

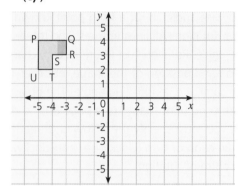

- Movement to the right (→) or up (↑) is positive.
- Movement to the left (←) or down (↓) is negative.

Translation only changes the position of the shape. Everything else stays the same, i.e. length and angle. The object and image are congruent shapes (see page 60).

Difficult translations can be completed more easily if you use tracing paper. Notice that all points (P', Q', R', S', T' and U') in the following example have moved 6 to the right and 7 down.

① This shape must be translated using the translation vector $\begin{pmatrix} 6 \\ -7 \end{pmatrix}$.

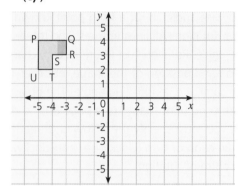

② Trace the shape onto tracing paper.

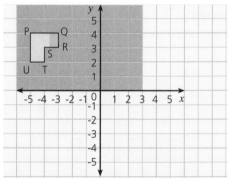

③ Place the tracing paper in the correct position using any point, e.g. Q.

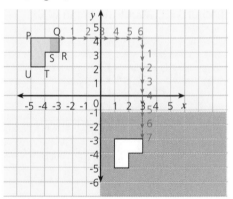

④ Draw over the image, first checking that it is correct.

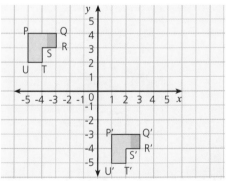

Enlargement

An enlargement changes the size of a shape. The shape can be made bigger or smaller according to the scale factor. All enlargements take place from one point called the centre of enlargement.

To describe an enlargement you must specify the following two things:

- The centre of enlargement
- The scale factor

Positive Scale Factor

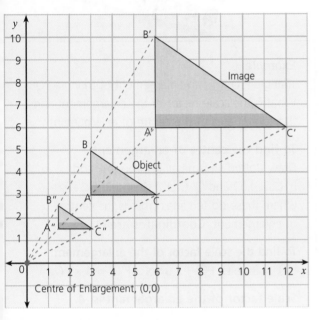

Centre of Enlargement, (0,0)

Positive Scale Factor Greater Than 1

A scale factor greater than 1 means that the size of the image is bigger than the size of the object. Triangle A'B'C' is an enlargement of triangle ABC by a scale factor of 2, centre (0,0).

A'B' = 2 x AB		OA' = 2 x OA
A'C' = 2 x AC	and	OB' = 2 x OB
B'C' = 2 x BC		OC' = 2 x OC

Positive Scale Factor Less Than 1

A scale factor less than 1 means that the size of the image is smaller than the size of the object. Triangle A''B''C'' is an 'enlargement' of Triangle ABC by a scale factor of $\frac{1}{2}$, centre (0,0).

A''B'' = $\frac{1}{2}$ x AB		OA'' = $\frac{1}{2}$ x OA
A''C'' = $\frac{1}{2}$ x AC	and	OB'' = $\frac{1}{2}$ x OB
B''C'' = $\frac{1}{2}$ x BC		OC'' = $\frac{1}{2}$ x OC

Enlargement only changes the size of the shape (i.e. the lengths of its sides) and its position.

Corresponding angles in the object and the image are the same, i.e. the shapes are similar. The orientation of the image is also the same as the object.

Sometimes you are asked to calculate the scale factor and find the centre of enlargement.

Example

Triangle P'Q'R' is an enlargement of triangle PQR. What is the scale factor of the enlargement and the coordinates of the centre of enlargement?

- **To find the centre of enlargement:**
  Draw dotted lines passing through
  P and P' (_____), Q and Q' (_____), R and R' (_____).
  Where these dotted lines cross is the centre of enlargement. **Coordinates are (0, 1).**
- **To find the scale factor of the enlargement:**
  P'Q' = 10 units
  PQ = 2 units
  $\therefore$P'Q' = 5 x PQ

Scale factor of the enlargement is 5.

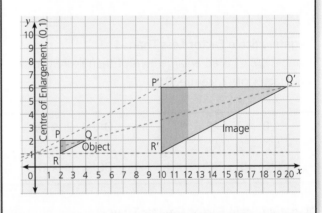

Note: the scale factor of an enlargement is a length scale factor. The scale factor for the area is different.

Area of triangle PQR = 1 square unit
Area of triangle P'Q'R' = 25 square units
Area scale factor = 25 = 5^2

In general, if the scale factor of an enlargement is k then the area scale factor is k^2.

Transformations

Enlargement with a Negative Scale Factor

With a negative scale factor, the number tells us if the shape is to be made bigger or smaller, while the negative sign tells us that the image and object are on opposite sides of the centre of enlargement.

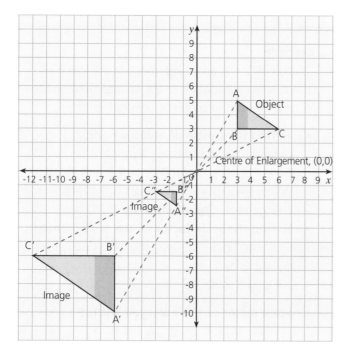

Negative Scale Factor Less Than -1

Triangle A'B'C' is an enlargement of triangle ABC by a scale factor of -2, centre (0,0).

A'B' = 2 × AB		OA' = 2 × OA
A'C' = 2 × AC	and	OB' = 2 × OB
B'C' = 2 × BC		OC' = 2 × OC

Negative Scale Factor Greater Than -1

Triangle A"B"C" is an 'enlargement' of triangle ABC by a scale factor of $-\frac{1}{2}$, centre (0,0).

A"B" = $\frac{1}{2}$ × AB		OA" = $\frac{1}{2}$ × OA
A"C" = $\frac{1}{2}$ × AC	and	OB" = $\frac{1}{2}$ × OB
B"C" = $\frac{1}{2}$ × BC		OC" = $\frac{1}{2}$ × OC

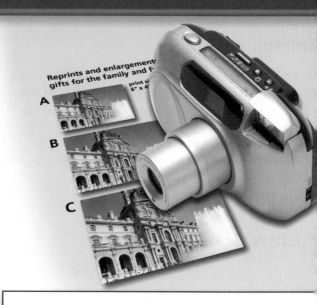

Example

Triangle P'Q'R' is an enlargement of triangle PQR. What is the scale factor of the enlargement and the coordinates of the centre of enlargement?

To find the centre of enlargement:
Draw dotted lines passing through P and P' (_____), Q and Q' (_____), R and R' (_____), where these dotted lines cross is the centre of enlargement. **Coordinates are (1,0)**

To find the scale factor of the enlargement:
P'Q' = 8 units, PQ = 2 units ∴ P'Q' = 4 × PQ.

Scale factor of the enlargement is -4.

Remember it is negative since the image and the object are on opposite sides of the centre of enlargement.

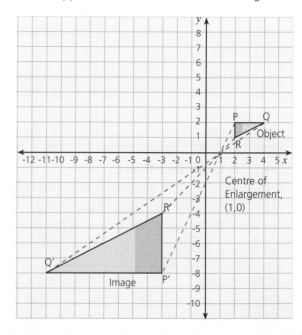

Transformations

Combination of Transformations

Very often a combination of two (or more) transformations can be described by a single transformation.

Examples

1 Triangle ABC is reflected in the *y*-axis to A'B'C' and then A'B'C' is reflected in the *x*-axis to A''B''C''.

Draw the two transformations and describe fully the single transformation that maps triangle ABC onto triangle A''B''C''.

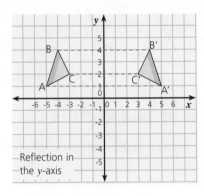

Reflection in the *y*-axis

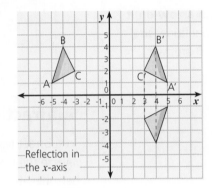

Reflection in the *x*-axis

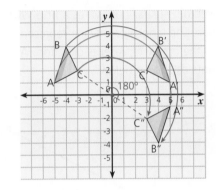

The single transformation is a rotation of 180° about the origin

2 Shape A is rotated 90° clockwise about the origin to shape B. Shape B is then reflected in the *x*-axis to shape C.

Draw the two transformations and describe fully the single transformation that maps shape A onto shape C.

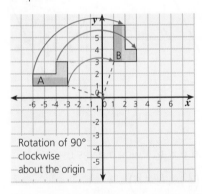

Rotation of 90° clockwise about the origin

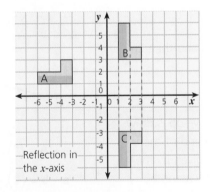

Reflection in the *x*-axis

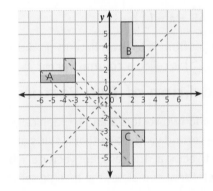

The single transformation is a reflection in the line $y = x$

A Summary of the Characteristics of Transformations

Transformation / Characteristic	You need to specify...	Properties that are preserved	Properties that change	Congruent or Similar?
Reflection	• The mirror line (equation of the line of reflection)	Shape and size (e.g. angles, lengths of sides)	Orientation, position	Congruent
Rotation	• Direction of turn • Centre of Rotation • Angle turned through	Shape and size (e.g. angles, lengths of sides)	Orientation, position	Congruent
Translation	• Direction of movement • Distance moved	Shape and size (e.g. angles, lengths of sides) and orientation	Position	Congruent
Enlargement	• Centre of Enlargement • Scale Factor	Angles, ratios of lengths of sides, orientation	Position, size	Similar

Vectors

Vectors

Vectors are quantities that have both **magnitude** (or size) and **direction**.

A common example of a vector quantity is displacement, which is distance moved in a particular direction. Another example is velocity, which is speed in a particular direction.

A vector is usually drawn as a **line with an arrow on it**, where the length of the line represents magnitude (size) and the arrow represents direction. **A** and **B** are two points as shown below.

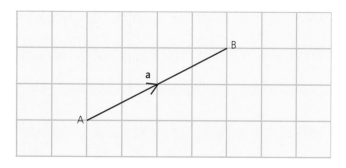

The displacement of **A** to **B** can be described in the following way:

$$\overrightarrow{AB} = \mathbf{a} = \begin{pmatrix} 4 \\ 2 \end{pmatrix}$$

To get from A to B we have to go 4 across and then 2 up. $\begin{pmatrix} 4 \\ 2 \end{pmatrix}$ is called a **column vector**.

Addition of Two Vectors

To add two vectors **a** and **b** graphically all we do is draw the second vector **b** so that it starts at the end of the first vector **a**. The resultant vector **a + b** is given by the vector that completes the triangle set up by **a** and **b**.

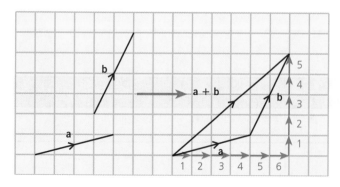

$$\mathbf{a} = \begin{pmatrix} 4 \\ 1 \end{pmatrix} \text{ and } \mathbf{b} = \begin{pmatrix} 2 \\ 4 \end{pmatrix} \text{ which gives us...}$$

$$\mathbf{a} + \mathbf{b} = \begin{pmatrix} 4 \\ 1 \end{pmatrix} + \begin{pmatrix} 2 \\ 4 \end{pmatrix} = \begin{pmatrix} 4+2 \\ 1+4 \end{pmatrix} = \begin{pmatrix} 6 \\ 5 \end{pmatrix}$$

The resultant of the addition of vectors **a** and **b** can also be thought of as the vector **a + b** along the diagonal SQ of the parallelogram PQRS as shown in this diagram.

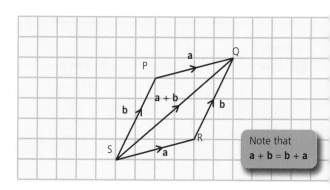

Note that
a + b = b + a

Subtraction of Two Vectors

To subtract two vectors **a** and **b** graphically you firstly reverse the direction of the second vector so that **b** now becomes **-b**. Draw **-b** so that it starts at the end of **a**. The resultant vector **a − b** is again given by the vector that completes the triangle set up by **a** and **-b**.

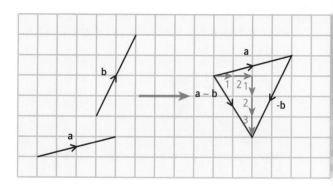

Also, $\mathbf{a} = \begin{pmatrix} 4 \\ 1 \end{pmatrix}$ and $\mathbf{b} = \begin{pmatrix} 2 \\ 4 \end{pmatrix}$ which gives us:

$$\mathbf{a} - \mathbf{b} = \begin{pmatrix} 4 \\ 1 \end{pmatrix} - \begin{pmatrix} 2 \\ 4 \end{pmatrix} = \begin{pmatrix} 4-2 \\ 1-4 \end{pmatrix} = \begin{pmatrix} 2 \\ -3 \end{pmatrix}$$

The resultant of the subtraction of vectors **a** and **b** can also be thought of as the vector **a − b** along the diagonal SQ of the parallelogram PQRS as shown in this diagram.

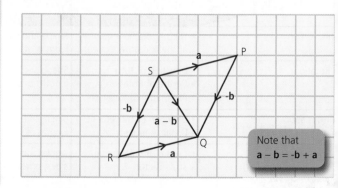

Note that
a − b = -b + a

Vector Proofs and 3-D Coordinates

Vectors may be used to prove some results in geometry.
This is something that may be required in an exam question.

Examples

1 In triangle ABC, G is the midpoint of AB and H is the midpoint of AC. If $\overrightarrow{AG} = \mathbf{a}$ and $\overrightarrow{AH} = \mathbf{b}$...

a) Find expressions for $\overrightarrow{BC}$ and $\overrightarrow{GH}$ in terms of $\mathbf{a}$ and $\mathbf{b}$.

b) Using your answers to part **a)** what two things can you prove about BC and GH?

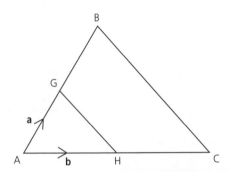

a) $\overrightarrow{BC} = \overrightarrow{BA} + \overrightarrow{AC}$

$\quad = -2\mathbf{a} + 2\mathbf{b}$

> To get from B to C we have to go from B to A ($\overrightarrow{BA}$) and then from A to C ($\overrightarrow{AC}$).
> Also $\overrightarrow{BA} = -\overrightarrow{AB} = -2\mathbf{a}$

$\overrightarrow{GH} = \overrightarrow{GA} + \overrightarrow{AH}$

$\quad = -\mathbf{a} + \mathbf{b}$

b) Since...

$\overrightarrow{GH} = -\mathbf{a} + \mathbf{b}$

and

$\overrightarrow{BC} = -2\mathbf{a} + 2\mathbf{b}$

$\quad = 2(-\mathbf{a} + \mathbf{b})$

$\quad = 2\overrightarrow{GH}$

This proves that...

i) BC has twice the length of GH

ii) BC and GH are parallel.

2 P, Q, R and S are the midpoints of sides AB, BC, CD and DA of quadrilateral ABCD respectively.
If $\overrightarrow{AB} = \mathbf{a}$, $\overrightarrow{AC} = \mathbf{b}$ and $\overrightarrow{AD} = \mathbf{c}$, prove that PQRS is a parallelogram.

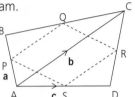

PQRS is a parallelogram providing that we can prove that PQ and SR are equal in length and parallel.

Firstly, let us determine $\overrightarrow{BC}$ and $\overrightarrow{DC}$ in terms of $\mathbf{a}$, $\mathbf{b}$ and $\mathbf{c}$.

$\overrightarrow{BC} = \overrightarrow{BA} + \overrightarrow{AC}$ and $\overrightarrow{DC} = \overrightarrow{DA} + \overrightarrow{AC}$

$\quad = -\mathbf{a} + \mathbf{b}$ $= -\mathbf{c} + \mathbf{b}$

We will now prove that $\overrightarrow{PQ} = \overrightarrow{SR}$:

$\overrightarrow{PQ} = \overrightarrow{PB} + \overrightarrow{BQ}$

$\quad = \tfrac{1}{2}\overrightarrow{AB} + \tfrac{1}{2}\overrightarrow{BC}$

$\quad = \tfrac{1}{2}\mathbf{a} + \tfrac{1}{2}(-\mathbf{a} + \mathbf{b})$

$\quad = \tfrac{1}{2}\mathbf{a} - \tfrac{1}{2}\mathbf{a} + \tfrac{1}{2}\mathbf{b} = \tfrac{1}{2}\mathbf{b}$

$\overrightarrow{SR} = \overrightarrow{SD} + \overrightarrow{DR}$

$\quad = \tfrac{1}{2}\overrightarrow{AD} + \tfrac{1}{2}\overrightarrow{DC}$

$\quad = \tfrac{1}{2}\mathbf{c} + \tfrac{1}{2}(-\mathbf{c} + \mathbf{b})$

$\quad = \tfrac{1}{2}\mathbf{c} - \tfrac{1}{2}\mathbf{c} + \tfrac{1}{2}\mathbf{b} = \tfrac{1}{2}\mathbf{b}$

$\overrightarrow{PQ} = \overrightarrow{SR}$, which means that PQ and SR are equal in length and are parallel; PQRS is therefore a parallelogram.

3-D Coordinates

Three coordinates are needed to identify a point in space, i.e. in 3-D (in three dimensions). Three axes each at right angles to each other are needed. The coordinates of each point represent distances from 0, a fixed point, firstly parallel to the x-axis then parallel to the y-axis, and finally parallel to the z-axis.

Examples

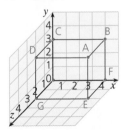

> Point A is (4,3,2) since we need to go 4 units parallel to the x-axis, then 3 units parallel to the y-axis and finally 2 units parallel to the z-axis.

Constructions

Construction of Triangles

In your exams, you must show all construction lines.

3 sides given: Construct the triangle ABC where AB = 3cm, BC = 2.5cm and AC = 2cm

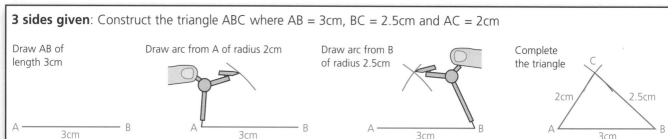

Draw AB of length 3cm

Draw arc from A of radius 2cm

Draw arc from B of radius 2.5cm

Complete the triangle

2 sides and the included angle given: Construct the triangle ABC where AB = 3cm, AC = 2cm and BÂC = 70°

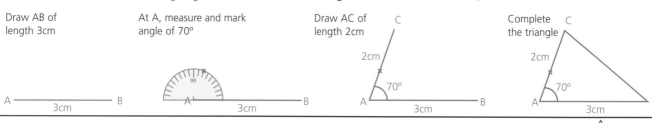

Draw AB of length 3cm

At A, measure and mark angle of 70°

Draw AC of length 2cm

Complete the triangle

2 sides and the non-included angle given: Construct the triangle ABC where AB = 2cm, AC = 2cm and AB̂C = 50°

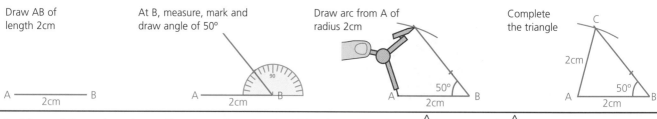

Draw AB of length 2cm

At B, measure, mark and draw angle of 50°

Draw arc from A of radius 2cm

Complete the triangle

1 side and 2 angles given: Construct the triangle ABC where AB = 3cm, BÂC = 50° and AB̂C = 30°

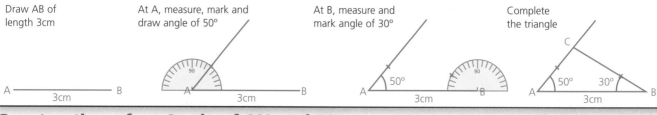

Draw AB of length 3cm

At A, measure, mark and draw angle of 50°

At B, measure and mark angle of 30°

Complete the triangle

Construction of an Angle of 60° and 90°

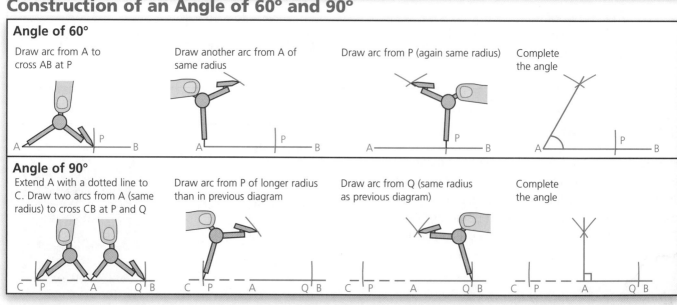

Angle of 60°

Draw arc from A to cross AB at P

Draw another arc from A of same radius

Draw arc from P (again same radius)

Complete the angle

Angle of 90°

Extend A with a dotted line to C. Draw two arcs from A (same radius) to cross CB at P and Q

Draw arc from P of longer radius than in previous diagram

Draw arc from Q (same radius as previous diagram)

Complete the angle

Constructions

The Midpoint and Perpendicular Bisector of a Line Segment

Draw arcs of equal radius from points A and B to intersect at C.

Draw arcs of the same radius on the other side of the line to intersect at D.

Join C to D to form the perpendicular bisector (or to locate the midpoint).

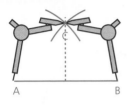

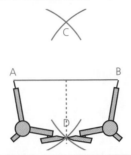

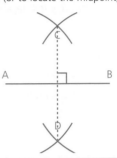

The Perpendicular from a Point to a Line

Draw two arcs from 0 to cross AB at P and Q.

Draw arc from P.

Draw arc from Q (using same radius as previous diagram).

Complete the perpendicular.

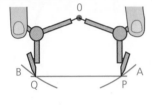

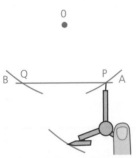

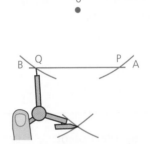

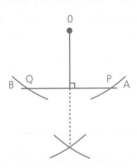

The Perpendicular from a Point on a Line

Draw arcs of equal radius from point 0, to cross AB at P and Q.

Draw arcs of the same radius (but greater than step 1) from P and Q to intersect at R.

Join 0 to R to form the perpendicular from point 0.

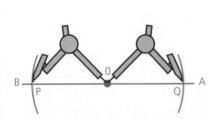

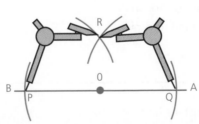

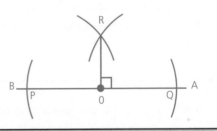

The Bisector of an Angle

This construction may be combined with the construction of angles 60° and 90° to give angles of 30° and 45°.

Draw arcs of equal radius from point A to cut lines at B and C.

Draw arcs of equal radius from points B and C to intersect at point D.

Join A to D to form the bisector of the angle.

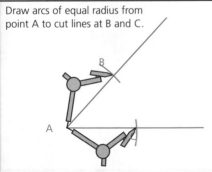

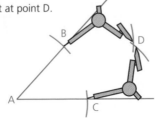

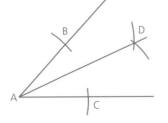

Loci

Locus

A locus is a set of points that satisfy some condition. Depending on the condition, the set of points may lie on a line or cover an area inside a shape.

The locus of points that are always at a constant distance from a point is a circle whose radius is equal to the constant distance.

The locus of points that are always at a constant distance from a line is a pair of parallel lines, one above and one below the line with a pair of semi-circles, one at each end of the line.

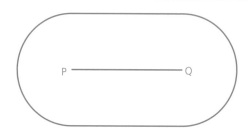

The locus of points that are always equidistant from two points is a line that bisects the line between the two points at right angles (i.e. a perpendicular bisector).

The locus of points that are further from P than Q lie in the region to the right of the perpendicular bisector. In this case, the line itself would be shown dotted to show that it is not included.

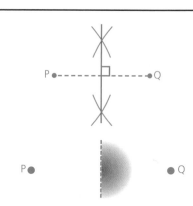

The locus of points that are always equidistant from two diverging lines is a line that bisects the angle between the two lines (i.e. an angle bisector).

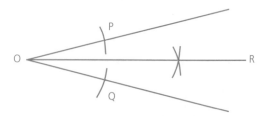

The locus of points closer to OP than OQ lie above OR. Again, the line itself would be shown dotted to show that it is not included.

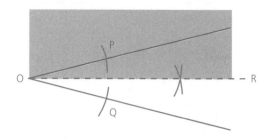

Perimeter and Circumference

Perimeter

Perimeter is the distance all the way around the outside of a shape. It is measured in units of length such as cm or m.

Example

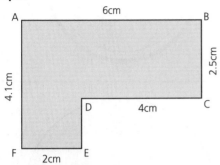

The lengths of all the sides are given or can be worked out and so...

Perimeter = AB + BC + CD + DE + EF + FA
= 6 + 2.5 + 4 + (4.1 − 2.5) + 2 + 4.1
= **20.2cm**

OR BC + DE = 4.1cm
Perimeter = 2 × 6cm + 2 × 4.1cm
= 12cm + 8.2cm
= **20.2cm**

Circumference of a Circle

Circumference is the mathematical word for the perimeter of a circle. The **radius** is the distance from the centre, ● , to the outside of the circle. The **diameter** is the distance from one side of the circle through the centre, ● , to the other side of the circle, which therefore means that...

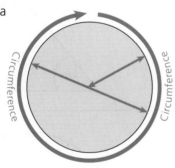

radius = $\frac{1}{2}$ × diameter $r = \frac{1}{2}d$
or diameter = 2 × radius $d = 2r$

The circumference of a circle is given by...

circumference = π × diameter $C = \pi d$
or circumference = 2 × π × radius $C = 2\pi r$

Examples

1 Calculate the circumference of this circle (to 3 s.f.).
Use π = 3.14

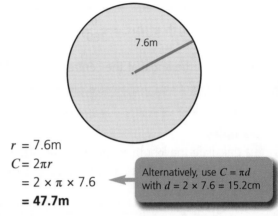

$r = 7.6$m
$C = 2\pi r$
$= 2 \times \pi \times 7.6$
$= \mathbf{47.7m}$

> Alternatively, use $C = \pi d$
> with $d = 2 \times 7.6 = 15.2$cm

2 This shape is made from semi-circles.
Calculate the distance from A to B along the curve (to 3 s.f.).

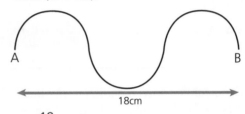

$d = \dfrac{18}{3} = 6$cm

$C = \pi d = \pi \times 6$

A to B = $1.5C$
A to B = $1.5 \times \pi \times 6$
$= 28.274...$
$= \mathbf{28.3cm}$

3 Find an exact expression in terms of π for the perimeter of the diagram below.

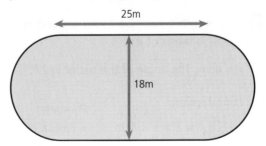

Perimeter
= circumference of circle + lengths of straight sides
$= (\pi \times 18) + (2 \times 25)$
$= \mathbf{(18\pi + 50)m}$

Arcs and Circumference

Length of an Arc

An arc is simply part of the circumference of a circle.

The length of an arc is given by:

> **Length of Arc** $= \dfrac{\theta}{360°} \times 2\pi r$
>
> Where θ is the angle at the centre of the circle.

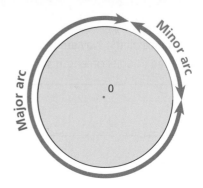

Major arc

Minor arc

0

Examples

1 Calculate the length of the minor arc **AB** in the following diagram (to 3 s.f.) using $\pi \approx 3.14$

Length of minor arc

$= \dfrac{50°}{360°} \times 2\pi r$

$= \dfrac{50}{360} \times 2 \times \pi \times 5\text{cm}$

$= 4.361\ldots \text{ cm}$

$= \mathbf{4.36cm}$ ← Round your answer at the end

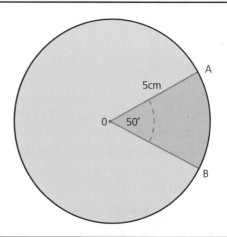

A

5cm

0 ◄ 50°

B

2 The diagram shows a garden flower bed in the shape of a sector of a circle. Use the π button on your calculator.
Calculate its perimeter (to 2 d.p.).

Press + 2 × 9.82 to continue the calculation on your **calculator**

Length of arc

$= \dfrac{48°}{360°} \times 2 \times \pi \times 9.82\text{m}$

$= \dfrac{48}{360} \times 2 \times \pi \times 9.82\text{m}$

$= 8.226\text{m}$ (to 4 s.f.)

Perimeter

$= \text{length of arc} + 2 \times 9.82\text{m}$

$= 8.226\ldots + 2 \times 9.82\text{m}$

$= 27.866\ldots \text{ m}$

$= \mathbf{27.87m}$

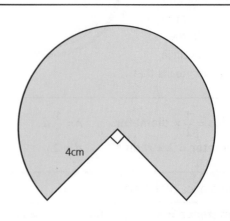

48°

9.82m

3 Find an exact expression for the perimeter of this shape in terms of π.

$r = 4\text{cm}$, The angle of the sector is $270°$.

Length of arc

$= \dfrac{270°}{360°} \times 2 \times \pi \times 4\text{cm}$

$= \dfrac{3}{4} \times 2 \times \pi \times 4\text{cm}$

$= 6\pi\text{cm}$

Perimeter

$= \text{length of arc} + 8\text{cm}$

$= \mathbf{(6\pi + 8)cm}$

4cm

Area of Quadrilaterals

Area

Area is a measure of the amount of surface covered by a shape. Area is measured in square units, e.g. cm² (cm squared), or m² (m squared).

To find the area of a square, rectangle or parallelogram, use the following formula:

Area = Base x Height

Square

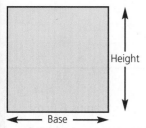

Rectangle

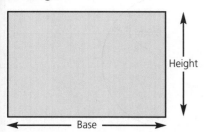

Parallelogram

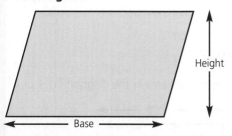

Trapezium

To find the area of a trapezium, use the following formula:

$$\text{Area} = \frac{1}{2}(a + b)\,h$$
$$\text{or...} = \frac{(a + b)}{2} \times h$$

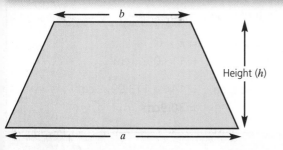

Examples

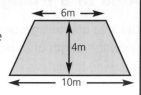

1 Calculate the area of the following trapezium.

Using our formula: $\text{Area} = \frac{(a + b)}{2} \times h$

$$\text{Area} = \frac{(10m + 6m)}{2} \times 4m$$

$$= \frac{16m}{2} \times 4m$$

$$= 8m \times 4m$$

$$= \textbf{32m}^2 \text{ (remember the units)}$$

2 The following parallelogram has an area of 24cm². Calculate its height if the length of its base is 10cm.

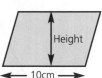

Using our formula: Area = Base × Height

$$24cm^2 = 10cm \times \text{Height}$$

$$\frac{24}{10} = \frac{\cancel{10}}{\cancel{10}} \times \text{Height}$$

> Divide both sides by 10 to give the height on its own

Height = 2.4cm (remember the units)

3 The diagram shows part of a kitchen wall that is to be tiled.

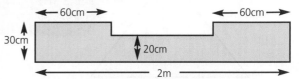

The tiles are 10cm square and are sold in boxes of 20. Each box costs £18.

a) Calculate the total cost of the tiles needed.

b) Calculate the cost per m² of using the tiles (to 2 d.p.).

a) The middle section of the wall has length
200cm − 60cm − 60cm = 80cm

Number of tiles needed = (6 × 3) + (8 × 2) + (6 × 3)
= 52

Number of boxes needed = 3
Total cost = 3 × £18 = **£54**

b) Area covered = (2m × 0.3m) − (0.8m × 0.1m)
= 0.52m²

Cost per m² = £54 ÷ 0.52 = £103.846...
= **£103.85** to the nearest penny

Area of Triangles and Circles

Area of a Triangle

The area of a triangle can be found very simply, if we know the length of its base and height, using the following formula:

$$\text{Area} = \frac{1}{2} \times \text{base} \times \text{height}$$
$$\text{or...} = \frac{\text{base} \times \text{height}}{2}$$

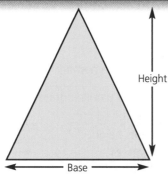
Height
Base

However, we can also work out its area if we know the length of two of the sides and their included angle. The formula is:

$$\text{Area} = \frac{1}{2}\, ab\sin C$$

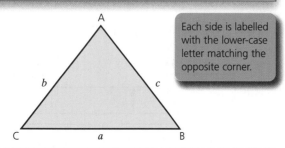

Each side is labelled with the lower-case letter matching the opposite corner.

Example

Calculate the area of the following triangle (to 3 s.f.):

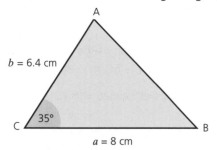

$b = 6.4$ cm
$a = 8$ cm
$35°$

$$\text{Area} = \frac{1}{2}\, ab\sin C$$
$$= \frac{1}{2} \times 8 \times 6.4 \times \sin 35° \text{ cm}^2$$
$$= 14.68... \text{ cm}^2$$
$$= \mathbf{14.7cm^2}$$

Area of a Circle

The area of a circle is given by the formula:

$$\text{Area} = \pi r^2$$

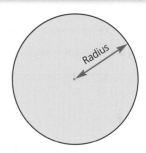
Radius

Examples

1 Calculate the area of a circle of radius 8.6cm (to 3 s.f.). Use the π button on your calculator.

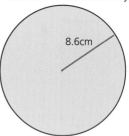
8.6cm

$$\text{Area} = \pi r^2$$
$$= \pi \times 8.6^2$$
$$= 232.35... \text{ cm}^2$$
$$= \mathbf{232cm^2}$$

2 Calculate the shaded area in the diagram (to 3 s.f.):

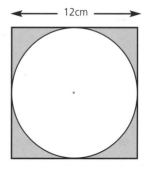
12cm

Area of square $= 12^2 = 144\text{cm}^2$

Area of circle $= \pi \times 6^2$
$= 113.09... \text{ cm}^2$

Shaded area $= 144 - 113.09... \text{ cm}^2$
$= \mathbf{30.9cm^2}$

Area of a Sector

A sector is the area enclosed by two radii and an arc. It can be major or minor.

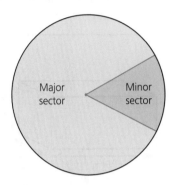

The area of a sector is given by:

Area of Sector = $\dfrac{\theta}{360°} \times \pi r^2$

where θ is the angle at the centre of the circle.

Example

Calculate the area of the minor sector in the following diagram (to 3 s.f.). Using $\pi = 3.14$

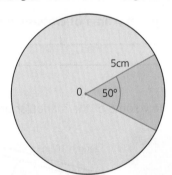

Area of Minor Sector $= \dfrac{\theta}{360°} \times \pi r^2$

$= \dfrac{50°}{360°} \times \pi \times 5^2$

$= \dfrac{50}{360} \times \pi \times 25$

$= 10.90...$ cm²

$= \textbf{10.9cm}^2$ **to 3 s.f.**

Surface Area of Solids

The surface area of any solid is simply the area of the **net** that can be folded to completely cover the outside of the solid (see page 69).

Examples

1. Calculate the surface area of the following triangular prism, which has an equilateral triangle as its cross-section.

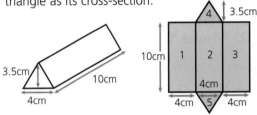

Area of 1 (Rectangle) = 10cm × 4cm = 40cm²
Therefore, Area of 1 + 2 + 3 = 120cm²

Area of 4 (Triangle) $= \dfrac{4\text{cm} \times 3.5\text{cm}}{2} = 7\text{cm}^2$

Therefore, Area of 5 = 7cm²

Surface Area of prism
= Area of 1 + 2 + 3 + 4 + 5
= 120cm² + 7cm² + 7cm²
= **134cm²** (remember the units)

2. Calculate the surface area of this cylinder (to 1 d.p.) using $\pi = 3.14$

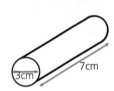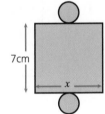

Area of each end $= \pi r^2$
= 3.14 × 1.5²
= 7.065cm²

Therefore, both ends
= 7.065 × 2 = 14.13cm²

Length of x = circumference of circle
= $2\pi r$
= 2 × 3.14 × 1.5
= 9.42cm

Therefore, area of rectangle
= 7 × 9.42
= 65.94cm²

Therefore, total area
= 14.13cm² + 65.94cm² = 80.07cm²
= **80.1cm²**

Volume

Volume

Volume is a measure of the amount of space a 3-D object takes up. It is usually measured in **units³**, e.g. **cm³** (cm cubed) or **m³** (m cubed).

Calculation of the Volume of a Solid Made Up of Cubes

Providing we know the volume of one cube, then all we have to do is work out how many cubes there are in each layer of the solid and then add them up.

Example
In the following example each cube has a volume of 1cm³.

This solid is made up of two layers

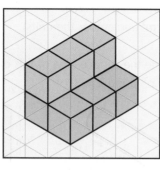

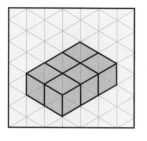 **+**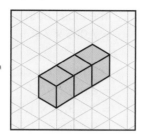

Bottom layer   Top layer

Volume = 6 cubes + 3 cubes
        = 6cm³ + 3cm³
        = **9cm³**

Volume of a Cuboid

> **Volume = Length × Width × Height**
> $$V = l \times w \times h$$

Example

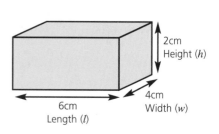

2cm
Height (h)

6cm
Length (l)

4cm
Width (w)

Using our formula:
Volume = length × width × height
        = 6cm × 4cm × 2cm
        = **48cm³** (remember the units)

Volume of a Prism

A prism is a solid which has a uniform cross-section from one end of the solid to the other end.

> **Volume of a prism = area of cross-section × length**

Example
Calculate the volume of the triangular prism.

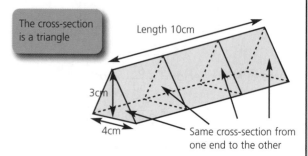

The cross-section is a triangle

Length 10cm

3cm

4cm

Same cross-section from one end to the other

Using our formula:
Volume = area of cross-section × length
        $= \dfrac{(\text{base} \times \text{height})}{2} \times \text{length}$
        $= \dfrac{(4\text{cm} \times 3\text{cm})}{2} \times 10\text{cm}$
        = 6cm² × 10cm

        = **60cm³** (remember the units)

Volume

Volume of a Cylinder

A cylinder is a prism that has a uniform cross-section of a circle from one end of the prism to the other. The volume of any cylinder is given by the formula:

> **Volume of a cylinder = $\pi r^2 l = \pi r^2 \times l$**
> **(where l is the length of the cylinder)**

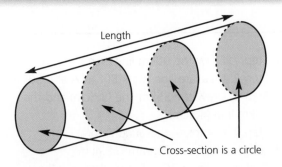

Length

Cross-section is a circle

Examples

1 Calculate the volume of the following cylinder (to 3 s.f.).

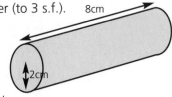

8cm

2cm

Using our formula:
Volume $= \pi r^2 l$
$= \pi \times 2^2 \times 8 \text{cm}^3$
$= 100.5... \text{cm}^3$
$= \mathbf{101 \text{cm}^3}$ **to 3 s.f.**

2 A cylindrical tank is 1.6m long and holds 0.8m³ of oil when full. What is the radius of the cylinder (to 3 s.f.).

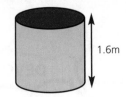

1.6m

Using our formula:
Volume $= \pi r^2 l$
$0.8 = \pi \times r^2 \times 1.6$
$\dfrac{0.8}{\pi \times 1.6} = r^2$
$0.1591... = r^2$
$r = \sqrt{0.1591...}$
$r = 0.3989...$
radius $= 0.399$cm

Volume of a Sphere

> **Volume $= \dfrac{4}{3} \times \pi \times (\text{radius})^3$**
> $= \dfrac{4}{3}\pi r^3$

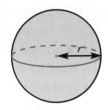

Volume of a Pyramid

> **Volume $= \dfrac{1}{3} \times$ Area of Base $\times$ Vertical Height**

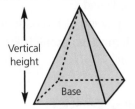 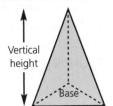

Vertical height

Base

Vertical height

Base

Volume of a Cone

> **Volume $= \dfrac{1}{3} \times$ Area of Base $\times$ Vertical Height**
> $= \dfrac{1}{3}\pi r^2 h$

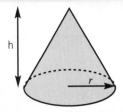

h

r

Example

Calculate the volume of the solid opposite (to 1 d.p.).

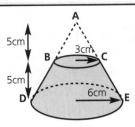

5cm

3cm

B   C

5cm

6cm

A

D   E

Volume of solid =
Volume of Cone **ADE** – Volume of Cone **ABC**
Volume of Cone **ADE** $= \dfrac{1}{3} \times \pi \times 6^2 \times 10$
$= 376.99... \text{cm}^3$

Volume of Cone **ABC** $= \dfrac{1}{3} \times \pi \times 3^2 \times 5$
$= 47.12... \text{cm}^3$

Volume of Solid $= 376.99\text{cm}^3 - 47.12\text{cm}^3$
$= 329.87\text{cm}^3$
$= \mathbf{329.9\text{cm}^3}$

Maps and Scale Drawings

Drawing to Size and Scale

Before you attempt to construct any drawing to a particular size or scale you need the following items:

- A **pencil** and **rubber** so any mistakes can be rubbed out.
- A **ruler** for drawing straight lines.
- A **protractor** for measuring angles.
- A **compass** for drawing circles, arcs and other constructions

---

Example

Here is a sketch map of an island. The map has four marker points A, B, C and D.

a) Make an accurate scale drawing of the quadrilateral ABCD using a scale of 1cm to represent 10km.

b) Calculate the length of BC.

a) Step 1: Draw the 90km line (9cm).
   Step 2: Measure and mark 80° at A and 90° at D.
   Step 3: Draw the 35km line (3.5cm) and the 45km line (4.5cm).
   Step 4: Complete the quadrilateral.

b) Length of BC on diagram = 8.4cm
   Real distance of BC = 8.4 × 10km = **84km**

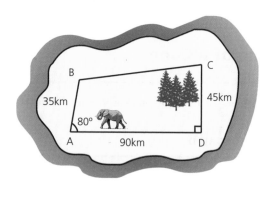

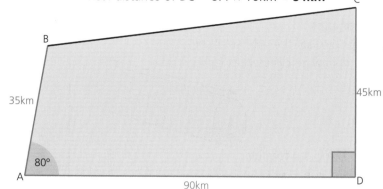

Map Scales

This is part of a map of Devon and Cornwall which is drawn to a scale of 1cm : 10km

1 The direct distance from Newquay to Plymouth as measured on the map is 7cm. Calculate the actual distance.

> Actual distance

= 7 × 10 = **70km**

2 The actual direct distance between Torquay and Exeter is 30km. Calculate the map distance.

> Map distance

$= \dfrac{30}{10} = \textbf{3cm}$

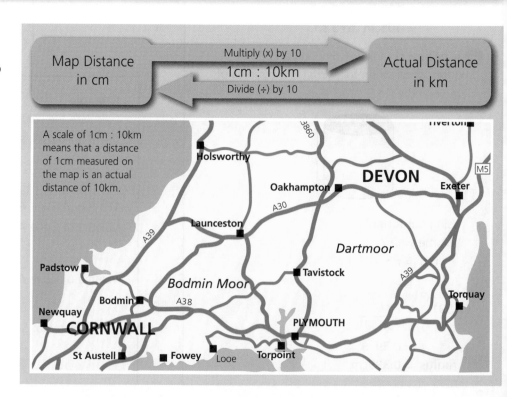

Effects of Enlargement

Similar Figures

Similar figures are identical in their shape but they are not identical in their size (they can be bigger or smaller). The two figures (cuboids) below are similar.

Figure A

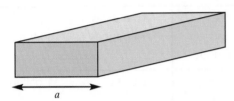

Figure B

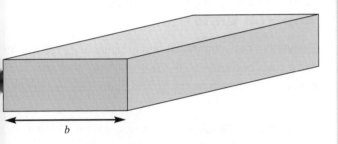

From our two figures:
The ratio of two corresponding lengths is $a : b$ (all other corresponding lengths will also be in the same ratio).

Since **area** is a measure of 'length squared', e.g. cm² or m², then the ratio of their areas is the ratio of the two corresponding lengths squared.

To put it simply…
Ratio of their areas = $a^2 : b^2$

Also, since **volume** is a measure of 'length cubed', e.g. cm³ or m³, then the ratio of their volumes is the ratio of the two corresponding lengths cubed.

To put it simply…
Ratio of their volumes = $a^3 : b^3$

Example
In Figure A opposite, a = 4cm and in Figure B opposite, b = 6cm. If the surface area of Figure A is 52cm² and its volume is 24cm³ calculate the surface area, and the volume of Figure B.

We know that…
Ratio of two corresponding lengths, $a : b$, is 4cm : 6cm which is the equal to 2 : 3

Ratio of areas $= a^2 : b^2$
$= 2^2 : 3^2$
$= 4 : 9$ (i.e. 4 parts to 9 parts)

For Figure A, 4 parts = 52cm²
1 part = $\frac{52}{4}$ = 13cm²

Figure B is equal to 9 parts
= 9 × 13cm²
= 117cm²

∴**Surface area of Figure B = 117cm²**

Ratio of volumes $= a^3 : b^3$
$= 2^3 : 3^3$
$= 8 : 27$

For Figure A, 8 parts = 24cm³
1 part = $\frac{24}{8}$ = 3cm³

Figure B is equal to 27 parts
= 27 × 3cm³
= 81cm³

∴**Volume of Figure B = 81cm³**

Two important notes:
① If the ratio of the area of two similar figures is for example 9 : 16 ($a^2 : b^2$) then the ratio of corresponding lengths will be $\sqrt{9} : \sqrt{16}$ = 3 : 4. This means that to go from area to length you must square root the ratio for area.
The ratio of their volumes will now be
$3^3 : 4^3$ = 27 : 64 ($a^3 : b^3$)

② If the ratio of the volume of two similar figures is for example 8 : 125 ($a^3 : b^3$) then the ratio of corresponding lengths will be $\sqrt[3]{8} : \sqrt[3]{125}$ = 2 : 5. This means that to go from volume to length you must cube root the ratio for volume.
The ratio of their areas will now be
$2^2 : 5^2$ = 4 : 25 ($a^2 : b^2$)

Converting Measurements

Metric and Imperial Units

	Metric Units		Approximate Comparison between Metric & Imperial		Imperial Units	
Length	10mm = 1cm 100cm = 1m 1000m = 1km		2.5cm ≈ 1 inch 1m ≈ 39 inches 1600m ≈ 1 mile 8km ≈ 5 miles		12 inches = 1 foot 3 feet = 1 yard 1760 yards = 1 mile	
Mass	1000mg = 1g 1000g = 1kg 1000kg = 1 tonne		30g ≈ 1 ounce 450g ≈ 1 pound 1kg ≈ 2.2 pounds		16 ounces = 1 pound 14 pounds = 1 stone	
Capacity or Volume	1000ml = 1l 1000cm³ = 1l (1ml = 1cm³)		1l ≈ $1\frac{3}{4}$ pints 4.5l ≈ 1 gallon		8 pints = 1 gallon	

Converting One Metric Unit to Another

Consider the conversion between centimetres (cm) and metres (m) as a typical example:

Divide (÷) by 100 as we are going from a bigger number (100) to a smaller number (1)

100cm → 100cm = 1m → 1m

Multiply (×) by 100 as we are going from a smaller number (1) to a bigger number (100)

Examples

1. Convert 300cm to metres.

 From above: cm $\xrightarrow{\div 100}$ m

 $300\text{cm} = \frac{300}{100} = 3\text{m}$

2. Penny is 1.65m tall. What is her height in centimetres?

 From above: m $\xrightarrow{\times 100}$ cm

 $1.65\text{m} = 1.65 \times 100 = \textbf{165cm}$

Converting Between Metric and Imperial Units

Converting between metric and imperial units follows the same rules because you divide or multiply. Take the conversion between grams (g) and pounds as an example:

Divide (÷) by 450 as we are going from a bigger number (450) to a smaller number (1)

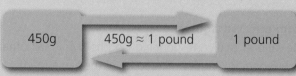

450g → 450g ≈ 1 pound → 1 pound

Multiply (×) by 450 as we are going from a smaller number (1) to a bigger number (450)

Examples

1. A tin of baked beans has a mass of 600g. What is its mass in pounds?

 From above: g $\xrightarrow{\div 450}$ pounds

 $600\text{g} = \frac{600}{450} = \textbf{1.33 pounds}$ (approx.)

2. A recipe for a cake needs 1.5 pounds of flour. What mass of flour is needed in grams?

 From above: pounds $\xrightarrow{\times 450}$ g

 $1.5 \text{ pounds} = 1.5 \times 450 = \textbf{675g}$ (approx.)

Bearings

Three-Figure Bearings

A bearing is a measurement of the position of one point relative to another point. It is measured in degrees. **Bearings are always measured from the north in a clockwise direction and are given as 3 digits**. Below are two points, A and B. There are two possible bearings:
- The bearing of B from point A. This means that the measurement of the bearing is taken **from point A**.
- The bearing of A from point B. This means that the measurement of the bearing is taken **from point B**.

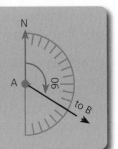

1. Draw in North (N) direction.
2. Measure angle from N direction in a clockwise direction.
3. Angle = 120°.
4. Bearing of B from A is 120°

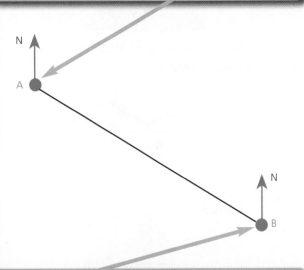

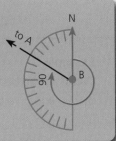

1. Draw in North (N) direction.
2. Measure angle from N direction in a clockwise direction.
3. Angle = 180° + 120° = 300°.
4. Bearing of A from B is 300°.

A circular protractor with a full 360° range can make three-figure bearings much easier to measure.

Sometimes the angle you measure from the N direction is less than 100° or even less than 10°. In this case one or two zeros are put in front of the angle in order to make them three-figure bearings.

Examples

1. Bearing of B from A is **075°**. (Also bearing of A from B is 255°). Use a protractor to check this bearing.

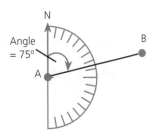

2. Bearing of B from A is **007°**. (Also bearing of A from B is 187°). Use a protractor to check this bearing.

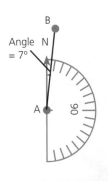

Compound Measures

Speed

Speed is a measure of 'how fast' an object is moving. To calculate the speed of a moving object we need two measurements:
- The **distance** it moves.
- The **time** it takes to move that distance.

Speed can be calculated using the following formula:

$$\text{Speed (S)} = \frac{\text{Distance (D)}}{\text{Time (T)}}$$

Speed is measured in metres per second (m/s), kilometres per hour (km/h) or miles per hour (mph).

A **formula triangle** makes it a lot easier for us when we want to calculate distance or time.

To get the formula for distance, cover 'D' up;
Distance = Speed × Time.

To get the formula for time, cover 'T' up;
Time = $\dfrac{\text{Distance}}{\text{Speed}}$

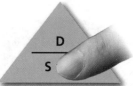

Examples
1. Calculate the speed of a car that travels a distance of 90m in 10s.

    Speed = $\dfrac{90m}{10s}$ = 9m/s (remember the units)

2. A train completes a journey of 150km at an average speed of 90km/h. How long did the journey take?

    Time = $\dfrac{\text{Distance}}{\text{Speed}}$ = $\dfrac{150km}{90km/h}$ = 1.6̇ hours

    $1\frac{2}{3}$ hours = 1 hour 40 minutes

Density

Density is a measure of 'how heavy' an object is 'per unit volume'. To calculate the density of an object we need two measurements:
- Its **mass**.
- Its **volume**.

Density can be calculated using the following formula:

$$\text{Density (D)} = \frac{\text{Mass (M)}}{\text{Volume (V)}}$$

Density is measured in grams per centimetre cubed, (g/cm³) or kilograms per metre cubed, (kg/m³).

A **formula triangle** makes it a lot easier for us when we want to calculate mass or volume.

To get the formula for mass, cover 'M' up;
Mass = Density × Volume.

To get the formula for volume, cover 'V' up;
Volume = $\dfrac{\text{Mass}}{\text{Density}}$

Example
Calculate the density of an object that has a mass of 75g and a volume of 100cm³.

Density = $\dfrac{75g}{100cm^3}$ = **0.75g/cm³** (remember the units)

Probability

The Nature of Probability

Probability is a measure of the likelihood that an event will occur.

To gain a good understanding of probability you need to learn the vocabulary used to describe it. This section covers the basic vocabulary within the context of examples.

Equally Likely Outcomes

Example
The 12 coloured counters shown below are put into a bag and one is selected at random.

Because the counters are all the same size and shape, each one has an **equal chance** of being selected. The selection of a particular counter is called an **outcome**. In this case, there are 12 **equally likely outcomes** and we say that a counter is to be selected at **random**.

For example, there are five red counters so five of the possible outcomes are associated with the **event** of selecting a red counter. In general, an event involves some set of outcomes and we talk about the probability of an event, written as P(event).

When all of the outcomes are equally likely, the probability of an event is given by:

$$P(event) = \frac{\text{Number of outcomes in the event}}{\text{The total number of outcomes}}$$

Using R to represent the selection of a red counter:
$$P(R) = \frac{5}{12}$$

In the same way, $P(B) = \frac{4}{12}$ and $P(Y) = \frac{3}{12}$

Using R' to represent the event of **not** selecting a red counter gives
$$P(R') = \frac{7}{12}$$ ← 7 counters are not red

Notice that $P(R') = 1 - P(R)$.

As a general result…

> For an event A, we use A' to represent the event that does not occur

$$P(A') = 1 - P(A)$$

Mutually Exclusive Events

Mutually exclusive events are events that have no outcomes in common. The events R (Red), B (Blue) and Y (Yellow) given opposite are mutually exclusive because every counter has only one colour.

$$P(R \text{ or } Y) = \frac{8}{12}$$ ← 8 counters are red or yellow

Notice that P(R or Y) = P(R) + P(Y)

In general, For mutually exclusive events A and B:

$$\textbf{P(A or B) = P(A) + P(B)}$$

We also have $P(R \text{ or } B \text{ or } Y) = \frac{12}{12} = 1$

In general, the sum of the probabilities of a complete set of mutually exclusive outcomes is **always 1**.

If A and B are **not** mutually exclusive events then P(A or B) is **not** equal to P(A) + P(B).

Example
A fair dice is rolled.
Let E be the event of obtaining an even score.
Let S be the event of obtaining a square number.

$$P(E) = \frac{3}{6} \qquad P(S) = \frac{2}{6}$$ ← E and S have 4 as a common outcome

$$P(E \text{ or } S) = \frac{4}{6} \neq \frac{3}{6} + \frac{2}{6} \,.$$

Probability

Outcomes of Single Events

- Tossing a coin – here there are only two outcomes: Heads or Tails
- Throwing a die – here there are only six outcomes: One, Two, Three, Four, Five or Six

In cases like these, all you have to do is make a simple list.

Outcomes of Two Successive Events

Tossing two coins, one after the other

In cases like these, it is easier to use a sample space diagram to show the possible outcomes.

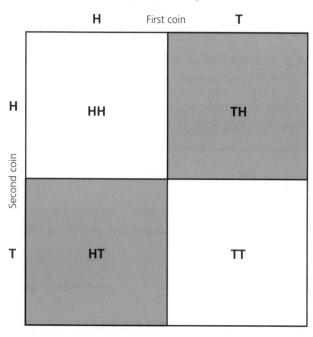

With two coins there are 4 outcomes. The chances of each outcome are…

$P(\text{Head + Head}) = \frac{1}{4}$

$P(\text{Tail + Tail}) = \frac{1}{4}$

$P(\text{Head + Tail}) = \frac{1}{4}$

$P(\text{Tail + Head}) = \frac{1}{4}$

Note that once again the probability of each outcome added together is 1,

i.e. $\frac{1}{4} + \frac{1}{4} + \frac{1}{4} + \frac{1}{4} = 1$

Throwing a pair of dice

In this case, each die has six possible outcomes. The sample space diagram, which shows the scores of the two dice added together, reveals a total of 36 possible outcomes.

Sample Space Diagram

First die

	1	2	3	4	5	6
1	2	3	4	5	6	7
2	3	4	5	6	7	8
3	4	5	6	7	8	9
4	5	6	7	8	9	10
5	6	7	8	9	10	11
6	7	8	9	10	11	12

Second die

Each outcome (e.g. throwing a 4 with the first die and a 2 with the second) has a $\frac{1}{36}$ **probability**.

However, while there is only a $\frac{1}{36}$ chance of scoring a total of either 2 or 12, there is a $\frac{6}{36}$ or $\frac{1}{6}$ chance of scoring a seven.

Independent Events

Independent events are events that have no influence or each other. For example, if a coin is flipped twice then whatever happens the first time does not affect what happens the second time. The two events are independent.

If A and B are two independent events then…

$$P(A \text{ and } B) = P(A) \times P(B)$$

This important rule only applies to independent events. The sample space diagram to the left shows, for example, that **P(HH) = ¼**. Notice that this fits the formula for independent events since…

$P(HH) = P(H) \times P(H) = \frac{1}{2} \times \frac{1}{2} = \frac{1}{4}$

Probability

Examples

1 A die and a coin are thrown. What is the probability of obtaining Heads and a score greater than 2?

Using H to represent Heads and S to represent a score greater than 2, the events H and S are independent.

$P(H) = \frac{1}{2}$

$P(S) = \frac{4}{6} = \frac{2}{3}$

P(H and S) = P(H) × P(S) $= \frac{1}{2} \times \frac{2}{3} = \frac{2}{6} = \frac{1}{3}$

We can also show this on a sample space diagram:

Die

		1	2	3	4	5	6
Coin	1	1,H	2,H	3,H	4,H	5,H	6,H
	2	1,T	2,T	3,T	4,T	5,T	6,T

The sample space contains 12 equally likely outcomes. 4 of the outcomes show Heads with a score greater than 2.
P(H and S) = $\frac{4}{12} = \frac{1}{3}$ as obtained using the rule for independent events.

2 What is the probability of throwing a 1 or a 2 with a die and picking a red or a green ball from inside a bag, which contains 4 black, 5 red and 3 green balls?

Throwing the die…
Let S represent the event of scoring 1 or 2 with the die and C represent the event of picking a red or green ball.

$P(S) = \frac{2}{6} = \frac{1}{3}$

$P(C) = \frac{8}{12} = \frac{2}{3}$

The events S and C are independent so…

P(S and C) = P(S) × P(C) $= \frac{1}{3} \times \frac{2}{3} = \frac{2}{9}$

Conditional Probability

If A and B are *not* independent events, then the probability that A occurs followed by B is given by…

> **P(A then B) = P(A) x P(B given that A has occured)**

This is known as **conditional probability**.

Example
A bag contains 3 red socks and 2 blue socks. A sock is selected at random and not replaced, then a second sock is selected at random.

What is the probability that both socks are blue?

The probability that the first sock is blue is $\frac{2}{5}$.

Given that the first sock is blue, only 1 blue sock remains out of 4. The probability that the second sock is also blue must be $\frac{1}{4}$.

P(both blue) $= \frac{2}{5} \times \frac{1}{4} = \frac{2}{20} = \frac{1}{10}$

N.B. if the first sock was replaced then the events would be independent giving…

P(both blue) $= \frac{2}{5} \times \frac{2}{5} = \frac{4}{25}$

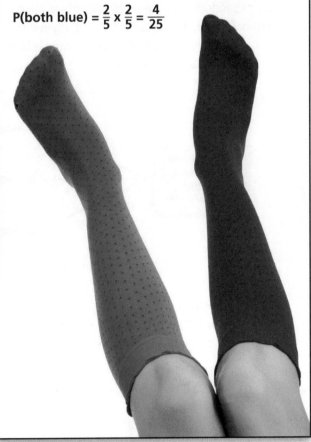

© iStockphoto / Thinkstock

Probability

Tree Diagrams

When dealing with the probability of a sequence of successive events, it is often better to use a tree diagram in order to simplify the task.

Examples

1 **Tossing Two Coins:** Each coin can give us two possible outcomes, a Head (**H**) or a Tail (**T**).

Calculate the probability of getting...
a) 2 Heads b) 2 Tails c) a Head and a Tail

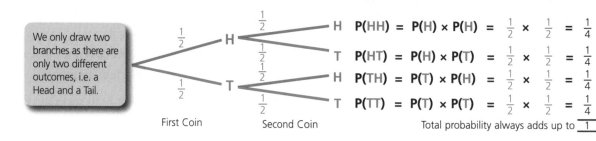

> We only draw two branches as there are only two different outcomes, i.e. a Head and a Tail.

First Coin   Second Coin

H   P(HH) = P(H) × P(H) = $\frac{1}{2}$ × $\frac{1}{2}$ = $\frac{1}{4}$

T   P(HT) = P(H) × P(T) = $\frac{1}{2}$ × $\frac{1}{2}$ = $\frac{1}{4}$

H   P(TH) = P(T) × P(H) = $\frac{1}{2}$ × $\frac{1}{2}$ = $\frac{1}{4}$

T   P(TT) = P(T) × P(T) = $\frac{1}{2}$ × $\frac{1}{2}$ = $\frac{1}{4}$

Total probability always adds up to __1__

a) P(HH) = $\frac{1}{4}$

b) P(TT) = $\frac{1}{4}$

c) P(HT) or P(TH) = $\frac{1}{4}$ + $\frac{1}{4}$ = $\frac{1}{2}$
(these are mutually exclusive outcomes)

2 From Jim's bag, the probability of selecting a red ball is 0.5, a blue ball is 0.3 and a green ball is 0.2. From Sandra's bag, the probability of selecting a red ball is 0.3, a blue ball is 0.3 and a green ball is 0.4. Jim selects a ball at random from his bag, followed by Sandra from hers.

Draw a tree diagram to show all the different outcomes. Then calculate the probability of selecting...
a) 2 Blues
b) 2 Reds or 2 Greens
c) Different colours

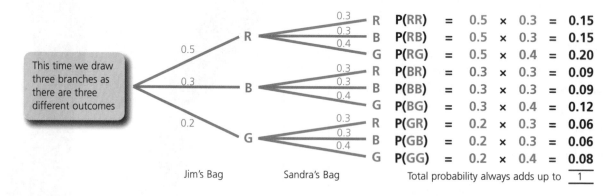

> This time we draw three branches as there are three different outcomes

Jim's Bag   Sandra's Bag

R   P(RR) = 0.5 × 0.3 = **0.15**
B   P(RB) = 0.5 × 0.3 = **0.15**
G   P(RG) = 0.5 × 0.4 = **0.20**
R   P(BR) = 0.3 × 0.3 = **0.09**
B   P(BB) = 0.3 × 0.3 = **0.09**
G   P(BG) = 0.3 × 0.4 = **0.12**
R   P(GR) = 0.2 × 0.3 = **0.06**
B   P(GB) = 0.2 × 0.3 = **0.06**
G   P(GG) = 0.2 × 0.4 = **0.08**

Total probability always adds up to __1__

a) P(BB) = 0.09

b) P(RR or GG) = 0.15 + 0.08 = 0.23
(these are mutually exclusive outcomes)

c) P(different colours)
= 1 – P (same colours)
= 1 – P (RR or BB or GG)
= 1 – (0.15 + 0.09 + 0.08) = 1 – 0.32
= **0.68**

Probability

Tree Diagrams (cont.)

Sometimes the probability of an event occurring depends on the outcome of a previous event. For example, a question may ask you to remove an object at random and then remove a second object at random. When this happens you must remember to adjust your probabilities for the second event.

This is known as conditional probability and a tree diagram, once again, is a useful tool for calculating probabilities based on these events.

Example

Jack's bag contains 10 balls of which 5 are red, 3 are blue and 2 are green. Jack picks a ball at random and, without replacing it, picks another ball at random.

Draw a tree diagram to show all the different possible outcomes. Use the diagram to calculate the probability of Jack picking balls that are…

a) the same colour

b) different colours

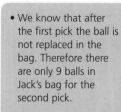

- We know that after the first pick the ball is not replaced in the bag. Therefore there are only 9 balls in Jack's bag for the second pick.

- If for example, the first pick is a red ball, then when the second pick is made there are only 4 red balls in the bag.

$$P(RR) = \frac{5}{10} \times \frac{4}{9} = \frac{20}{90}$$
$$P(RB) = \frac{5}{10} \times \frac{3}{9} = \frac{15}{90}$$
$$P(RG) = \frac{5}{10} \times \frac{2}{9} = \frac{10}{90}$$
$$P(BR) = \frac{3}{10} \times \frac{5}{9} = \frac{15}{90}$$
$$P(BB) = \frac{3}{10} \times \frac{2}{9} = \frac{6}{90}$$
$$P(BG) = \frac{3}{10} \times \frac{2}{9} = \frac{6}{90}$$
$$P(GR) = \frac{2}{10} \times \frac{5}{9} = \frac{10}{90}$$
$$P(GB) = \frac{2}{10} \times \frac{3}{9} = \frac{6}{90}$$
$$P(GG) = \frac{2}{10} \times \frac{1}{9} = \frac{2}{90}$$

First Pick   Second Pick   Total probability always adds up to 1

a) P(same colour)

= P(**RR** or **BB** or **GG**)

$$= \frac{20}{90} + \frac{6}{90} + \frac{2}{90} = \frac{28}{90}$$

$$= \frac{14}{45} \text{ (these are mutually exclusive outcomes)}$$

b) P(different colour)

= P(**RB** or **RG** or **BR** or **BG** or **GB** or **GR**)

$$= \frac{15}{90} + \frac{10}{90} + \frac{15}{90} + \frac{6}{90} + \frac{6}{90} + \frac{10}{90} = \frac{62}{90}$$

$$= \frac{31}{45} \text{ (these are mutually exclusive outcomes)}$$

Alternatively, **P(different colour)**

= 1 – P (same colour)

$$= 1 - \frac{14}{45} = \frac{31}{45}$$

Probability

Theoretical Probability

Since the chance of a coin landing on Heads is $\frac{1}{2}$, then the number of Heads we should expect in 10 tosses is…

$$\frac{1}{2} \times 10 = 5$$

The most likely number of heads is 5, but this is not certain.

Relative Frequency

Example

A simple experiment was carried out where a coin was tossed 10, 100 and a 1000 times. The graphs below show the number of Heads and Tails obtained. In theory we would expect to always get the same number of Heads and Tails because the probability of each event occurring is $\frac{1}{2}$ or 0.5

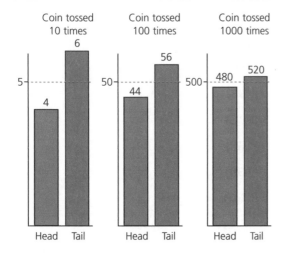

	Coin tossed 10 times	Coin tossed 100 times	Coin tossed 1000 times
Relative Frequency	Head = $\frac{4}{10}$ = 0.4	Head = $\frac{44}{100}$ = 0.44	Head = $\frac{480}{1000}$ = 0.48
	Tail = $\frac{6}{10}$ = 0.6	Tail = $\frac{56}{100}$ = 0.56	Tail = $\frac{520}{1000}$ = 0.52

The **relative frequency** of obtaining Heads (or Tails) in an experiment is given by…

$$\text{Relative Frequency} = \frac{\text{Number of Heads (or Tails) we get}}{\text{Total number of times the coin was tossed}}$$

If we go back to our experiment, as we increase the number of times the coin is tossed, the relative frequency gets closer and closer to the theoretical probability (red dotted line), e.g. 0.5 for a Head, 0.5 for a Tail.

Theoretical probability relates to equally likely outcomes. If this is not the case, such as when a coin is **biased**, we must use relative frequency to estimate probability.

Importance of Sample Size

As you can see from the example opposite, the bigger the sample, the more reliable it is.

For example, it is quite possible that tossing a coin ten times could produce 2 tails and 8 heads. A larger sample would give a more reliable result.

This has implications in testing for **bias**. For instance, it would be possible to test experimentally the frequency of red and black on a roulette wheel.

If there is time to take a big enough sample then it may be possible to say with some justification that the wheel is not fair, e.g. if 50 000 spins produce 26 750 reds and 23 250 blacks!

Problem Solving and Handling Data

Problem Solving in Statistics

You need to be aware of the problem solving process in statistics and how to use the handling data cycle.

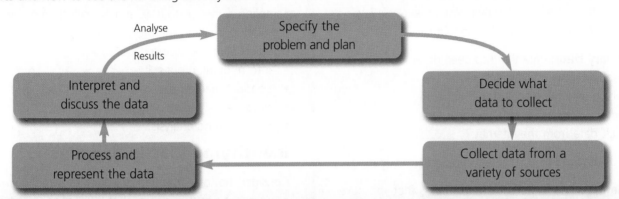

Stage	Examples
Specify the Problem and Plan You need to have a clear understanding of the problem to be solved. You then need to formulate some questions that will provide the necessary information to solve the problem. As the process develops, and information is gathered, further lines of enquiry may arise.	• Discuss what better concentration means and how it would be evident in a classroom. • Consider making some observations in lessons. • Which lessons would you observe? • Does the age of pupils make a difference? • Does the ability set make a difference?
Decide what Data to Collect You need to decide what data you will collect, how it will be collected and how much you will collect (sample size). Think about different types of data such as qualitative and quantitive, discrete and continuous.	• One possibility is to select some pupils in a class and observe them. • The lesson could be divided up into intervals in which these pupils are concentrating or not. • At the end of the lesson each pupil would have a total time. • Consider the use of secondary data.
Collect Data from a Variety of Sources Consider observations, experiments, surveys, and primary and secondary sources. Use suitable data collection techniques, such as the various sampling methods, and give thought to how you will record the data so that it will be easy to work with later.	• A suitable data sheet would be needed to use in the classroom observations. • It may be possible to research the subject on the Internet.
Process and Represent the Data Use relevant statistical measures that summarise the data and consider graphs and charts to represent it.	• You could calculate the mean concentration time for boys and for girls. • The data might be represented using box plots for example.
Interpret and Discuss the Data Consider the data in terms of the original problem and the questions asked. Decide whether the problem has been answered or if further lines of enquiry now need to be followed in a new cycle.	• Use the statistics calculated along with the charts to make comparisons and draw conclusions.
Possible follow-up enquiry	• Do girls / boys do better in single sex lessons / schools?

Collecting Data

Data Handling Definitions

Primary Data: data that has been directly obtained first hand, either by yourself or by someone under your direction. It can be collected by questionnaire, survey, observation, experiment or data logging.

Secondary Data: data that has been obtained independently by an external agency and which may be already stored either in printed or electronic form, e.g. published statistics, data from the Internet.

The Population: all of the items you are investigating.

The Sample: the limited number of items that you have selected to represent the whole population.

A Random Sample: a sample in which every item of the population has an equal chance of being selected. In practice this means taking great care to spread the 'randomness' over as large an area as possible and to take repeated surveys and work out averages.

A Stratified Sample: is a sample made up of distinct groups in the same proportions as they appear in the whole population.

Example
Suppose that a survey is to be carried out from a sample of 10% of the employees of a company employing 120 women and 31 men. A basic random sample would consist of 15 employees but may not have a representative proportion of men and women. A stratified sample would be made up of 12 women and 3 men selected at random.

Reasons for Sampling

Information is a hugely powerful tool in modern society but clearly it is impossible to survey huge populations. Sampling allows us to look at a cross-section of the population, making the process much quicker and much cheaper! Samples are used widely to…
- inform opinion polls
- conduct market research
- produce T.V. viewing figures
- provide trend analysis.

Identifying Bias in Samples

Consider the following bad examples of sampling:
- A recent survey suggests that 82% of the population prefer Rugby League to Football. The survey was conducted in St Helens.
- A High Street survey reveals that 76% of men aged between 18 and 42 go to the pub at least once a week. The survey was conducted at 11pm.
- A telephone survey suggests that 100% of the population has at least one telephone in their house.

In order to be unbiased, every individual in the population must have an equal chance of being included in the sample. This means taking into account…
- the time of day of the survey
- the age range
- relative affluence
- the geographical area
- ethnicity
- lifestyle.

However, you must also remember that the bigger the sample size, the more representative it is likely to be (assuming of course that you have minimised all the other potential areas of bias).

Collecting Data

Collecting Data by Observation

Collecting data by observation can be laborious and time consuming but for some things it is the best way. For instance, a traffic survey might be done in this way to reveal the volume of traffic using a bridge. You must remember to ask yourself whether the survey is being conducted at an appropriate time.

Collecting Data by Experiment

People involved in the Sciences use experiments to gather data to support their hypotheses. The key things to remember are that…

• the experiment must be repeated an appropriate number of times
• someone else should be able to repeat the experiment in the same way.

Collecting Data by Questionnaire

Questionnaires are skillfully designed forms, which are used to conduct surveys of a sample of the population.

Designing a Questionnaire

Good questionnaires have the following things in common:

• They are not too long, i.e. never more than 10 questions, but less if possible.
• They contain questions that are easily understood and do not cause confusion.
• They ask for simple, short answers, e.g. Yes/No, Like/Don't Like or Male/Female
• They avoid vague words like Tall, Old, Fast, Good, etc. The questions do not show any bias, e.g. 'Do you prefer watching rugby or hockey?' rather than 'Do you agree that rugby is a more watchable game than hockey?'
• They only contain relevant questions.

Example

Yasmin decides to test the hypothesis that 'Parents would prefer the school holidays to be shorter' by using the following questionnaire.

This tests whether the questionnaire is relevant to this person

The answer may be affected by the size of the family!

The answer may turn out to be dependent upon the age of the person's children!

This tells us whether or not the person will see a lot of his/her children over the holidays!

This avoids asking a 'loaded question', i.e. it avoids bias

QUESTIONNAIRE

1. Do you have children of school age?
   Yes ❑ No ❑

2. How many children do you have?
   1 ❑ 2 ❑ 3 ❑ 4+ ❑

3. To which age group do they belong?
   11-13 ❑ 14-16 ❑ 17-18 ❑

4. Are you in full time employment?
   Yes ❑ No ❑

5. Do you think the school holidays are…
   Too Short? ❑
   Too Long? ❑
   Just Right? ❑

From the answers, Yasmin could…
• reject any responses from people who aren't parents
• analyse the data to see if family size, age range and employment status affect the answers
• come up with a pretty good answer to her original hypothesis.

Sorting Data

Discrete and Continuous Data

Data comes in many different forms. To make sense of the data it is often sorted and collated. There are two different types of data that you can record for sorting and collating.

Discrete data can only have certain values. For example, the number of goals a football team can score in a match is 0, 1, 2, 3, 4, etc. They cannot have a score in between, like 0.5, 1.6, 2.2, etc.

Continuous data can have any value. It tends to be obtained by reading measuring instruments. The accuracy of the data is dependent on the precision of the equipment.

Tally Charts and Frequency Tables
Very often the best way to sort and collate discrete or continuous data is to draw a tally chart and a frequency table.

Example
Here are the results of the games involving Germany, the host nation, in Round 1 through to the semi-finals of a Hockey World Cup tournament.

Germany 4 Costa Rica 2	Germany 2 Sweden 0
Germany 1 Poland 0	Germany 4 Argentina 2
Germany 0 Brazil 3	Germany 0 Italy 2

Sort the number of goals scored per game by each team by drawing a tally chart and a frequency table.

Since the range of data here is narrow (e.g. from 0 to 4 goals scored) each value can be included individually in the tally chart and frequency table. As you complete the tally column, tick off each number as you go along. This makes sure that you do not include the same number twice or miss any out.

Germany 4̸ Costa Rica 2̸	Germany 2̸ Sweden 0̸
Germany 1̸ Poland 0̸	Germany 4̸ Argentina 2̸
Germany 0̸ Brazil 3̸	Germany 0̸ Italy 2̸

Number of goals scored	Tally	Frequency of that no. of goals being scored by a team
0	IIII	4
1	I	1
2	IIII	4
3	I	1
4	II	2
		Total = 12

The numbers in the frequency column are simply the number of tallies. Remember to add them up, as this total is equal to the total number of pieces of data (not, in this example, the total number of goals scored!).

N.B. The data in this example is discrete, however, the same process would apply for continuous data.

Sorting Data

Using Class Intervals

Sometimes, data is so widespread that it is impractical to include each value in the tally chart and frequency table individually. When this happens, the data is sorted into groups called class intervals, where each class interval represents a range of values.

Example

The newspaper cutting shows the recorded temperatures in °C for various places both at home and abroad. Sort the recorded temperatures, by drawing a tally chart and a frequency table.

Temperatures home and abroad

Amsterdam 19	Cairo 34	Majorca 27	New York 32
Athens 33	Cardiff 16	Manchester 12	Newcastle 13
Barbados 29	Dublin 15	Miami 26	Paris 20
Barcelona 26	Jersey 20	Milan 28	Peking 33
Berlin 23	London 21	Montreal 22	Prague 26
Bermuda 28	Madrid 33	Moscow 15	Rhodes 28

There is a wide range of data shown above, e.g. from 12°C to 34°C. Out of practicality, the temperature values are arranged in groups of five in our tally chart and frequency table.

The class interval $10 \leqslant T < 15$ would include any temperature reading equal to or greater than 10°C and less than 15°C (a temperature reading of 15°C is included in the next class interval) and so on.

Remember to total the numbers in the frequency column to make sure they add up to the total number of locations (pieces of data).

Recorded Temperatures, T(°C)	Tally	Frequency of Temperatures Falling Within that Range
$10 \leqslant T < 15$	II	2
$15 \leqslant T < 20$	IIII	4
$20 \leqslant T < 25$	⑷I	5
$25 \leqslant T < 30$	⑷I III	8
$30 \leqslant T < 35$	⑷I	5
		Total = 24

N.B. The data in this example is continuous, however, the same process would apply for discrete data

---

Two Important Points

- The format of class intervals can vary. The following class intervals could have been used to give the same results for the data above: 10–14, 15–19, 20–24, etc.
- The range of each class interval depends on the total range of the data. If the total range of the data is large and the range of each class interval is small, then your frequency table would have a lot of rows. Aim to have no more than 10 lines in your table!

Sorting Data

Stem and Leaf Diagrams

A stem and leaf diagram sorts data into groups.

One advantage of these diagrams over frequency tables is that they enable you to get more of a feel for the 'shape' of distribution.

> **Example**
>
> The following data shows the length of time (in minutes) it took 30 pupils to complete a test, arranged in ascending order:
>
> **8, 8, 9, 15, 15, 16, 16, 17, 18, 18, 20, 21, 21, 22, 23, 26, 27, 27, 28, 28, 29, 33, 34, 34, 35, 39, 39, 42, 48, 49.**
>
> This data can be represented using a stem and leaf diagram by taking the tens to form the 'stem' of the diagram and the units to form the 'leaves'.
>
> | 0 | 8 8 9 | Key: **1** **5** means **15** |
> |---|---|---|
> | **1** | 5 5 6 6 7 8 8 | |
> | **2** | 0 1 1 2 3 6 7 7 8 8 9 | |
> | **3** | 3 4 4 5 9 9 | |
> | **4** | 2 8 9 | |
> | Stem | Leaves | |

The end product is similar to a frequency table. However, besides allowing you to visualise the 'shape' of the data, it can be used to identify the modal class, i.e. the 20–29 group and the median, i.e. 24.5 (between the 15th and 16th piece of data as there are 30 values).

Notice that, in each row, the values are in order with the smallest in the left. This has happened because the original data was written in order. When the original data is not in order. It may be best to produce the stem and leaf diagram in two stages:

1 Use the data to produce an unordered stem and leaf diagram.

2 Order the numbers in each row.

Two-Way Tables

Two-way tables simply show two sets of information, one vertically and the other horizontally. Information organised in this way can actually result in you gaining more information than you started with.

> **Example**
>
> 'In a survey, 200 Year 7 and 8 pupils were asked if they preferred Maths or Science. 73 out of 110 Year 7 pupils preferred Maths, and in total 82 pupils preferred Science.' This could lead to the table below:
>
> | | Year 7 | Year 8 | Total |
> |---|---|---|---|
> | **Science** | | | 82 |
> | **Maths** | 73 | | |
> | **Total** | 110 | | 200 |
>
> … which in turn can be used to work out the missing data:
>
> | | Year 7 | Year 8 | Total |
> |---|---|---|---|
> | **Science** | 37 | 45 | 82 |
> | **Maths** | 73 | 45 | 118 |
> | **Total** | 110 | 90 | 200 |
>
> Notice that in the original table there was no data for Year 8 … now it's all there!

Various Types of Table

Tables can be arranged in many different ways to suit the purpose for which they are intended. Remember, the idea is to make the information as accessible as possible, so you've got to give a bit of thought as to how you want to present it.

Averages and Spread

Mean, Median, Mode and Range

The mean is given by the formula:

$$\text{Mean} = \frac{\text{Sum of the values}}{\text{Number of values}}$$

The **median** is the middle value once the data has been put in order of size. For an even number of values, add the middle pair and divide by 2 to find the median.

The **mode** is the most common data value, i.e. the one that occurs with the greatest frequency.

The **range** measures the spread of the data and is the difference between the smallest and largest data values.

Mean, Median, Mode and Range from a Frequency Table

Here is the frequency table (again) for the number of goals scored in games involving Germany, from Round 1 through to the semi-finals of the Hockey World Cup tournament.

The data in this frequency table is discrete.

Number of goals Scored (x)	Frequency (f)	Frequency × no. of goals Scored (fx)
0	4	4 × 0 = 0
1	1	1 × 1 = 1
2	4	4 × 2 = 8
3	1	1 × 3 = 3
4	2	2 × 4 = 8
	Total = 12	Total = 20

To calculate the **mean** we need to add another column (in green) to our frequency table to calculate the total number of goals scored.

$$\text{Mean} = \frac{\text{Total number of goals scored (f}x)}{\text{Total frequency}}$$
$$= \frac{20}{12} = 1.\dot{6} \text{ goals (per team per game)}$$

Mode = 0 and 2 goals
(because these occur more times than any of the others).

Since we have 12 pieces of data, the **median** number of goals is halfway between the 6th and 7th piece of data.

4 teams scored	1 team scored	4 teams scored	1 team scored	2 teams scored
0̸ 0̸ 0̸ 0̸	1̸	②② 2̸ 2̸	3̸	4̸ 4̸

Median = $\frac{2+2}{2}$ = **2 goals**

Range = 4 goals – 0 goals = **4 goals**

Mean, Median, Mode and Range from a Frequency Table of Grouped Data

Here is the frequency table for the recorded temperatures for various locations at home and abroad. The data in this frequency table is continuous.

Recorded Temp., T (°C)	Frequency (f)	Mid-Temp. Values (x)	Frequency × Mid-Temp. Values (fx)
10 ⩽ T < 15	2	12.5	2 × 12.5 = 25
15 ⩽ T < 20	4	17.5	4 × 17.5 = 70
20 ⩽ T < 25	5	22.5	5 × 22.5 = 112.5
25 ⩽ T < 30	8	27.5	8 × 27.5 = 220
30 ⩽ T < 35	5	32.5	5 × 32.5 = 162.5
	Total = 24		Total = 590

These are class intervals

These are halfway values for our class intervals

Estimated Mean

With grouped data, the individual values are unknown. Therefore we have to use 'mid-temperature value' to provide an **estimate** of the mean. To calculate the mean this time we need to add two further columns (in red) to our frequency table.

$$\text{Mean} = \frac{\text{Total of Recorded Temperatures (f}x)}{\text{Total Frequency}}$$
$$= \frac{590}{24}$$
$$= \textbf{24.58°C}$$

Mode

Again we don't get an exact mode but we are able to determine which class interval or group is the **modal class**. Modal Class is **25°C ⩽ T < 30°C** since this class interval has the highest frequency (i.e. it occurs the most number of times).

Median

With continuous data we don't get an exact value for the median, but we are able to determine which class interval or group it is in. The above table has 24 pieces of data and so the median is halfway between the 12th and 13th piece of data. Using the frequency column, the median is in the **25°C ⩽ T < 30°C** class interval.

Displaying Data

Displaying Data from a Table

The best way of displaying data that has been sorted into a frequency table is to draw a graph.

Here is the frequency table for the number of goals scored in games involving Germany in Round 1 through to the semi-finals of the Hockey World Cup (we only include the tally column when we are sorting the data).

No. of goals scored	0	1	2	3	4
Frequency	4	1	4	1	2

A Vertical Line Graph

This graph is very similar to the bar graph above, except that lines are drawn instead of bars. Make sure that the height of each line is equal to the correct frequency.

A Line Graph

This is not always the most suitable way to display discrete data, as the lines joining the points have no meaning!

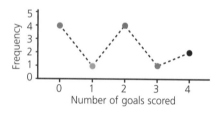

Dual and Composite Bar Charts

Data from two or more groups may be shown on a single chart. A **dual** bar chart shows the bars side by side and a **composite** bar chart combines the responses in a single bar. A key is needed to explain what each part of the chart represents.

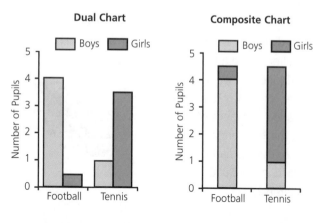

Displaying Grouped Data

Data that has been grouped together and sorted, using class intervals, in a frequency table can also be displayed by drawing a graph.

Here is the frequency table for the recorded temperatures for various locations at home and abroad.

Recorded Temperatures T(°C)	Frequency
$10 \leqslant T < 15$	2
$15 \leqslant T < 20$	4
$20 \leqslant T < 25$	5
$25 \leqslant T < 30$	8
$30 \leqslant T < 35$	5

The data above can be displayed in various ways:

A Frequency Diagram

A frequency diagram is very much like a bar graph, but since we have grouped data then the bars do not have a gap between them, i.e. they must be continuous.

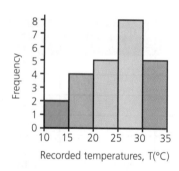

A Frequency Polygon

With a frequency polygon you need to mark the middle of the top of each bar in the frequency diagram with a cross and then join up these crosses with straight lines.

You may be asked to draw a frequency polygon directly from the frequency table. You must remember to plot the crosses at the correct frequency exactly over the middle of the class intervals, e.g. for **$10 \leqslant T < 15$**, plot the cross above 12.5

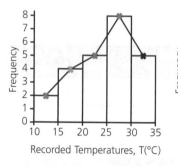

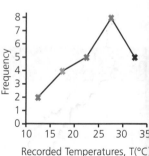

Displaying Data

Histograms

Frequency graphs for grouped continuous data, where the **area** of each column represents the frequency of that class interval, are called histograms.

Example
The frequency table below shows the distribution of the ages of the people in a supermarket at a particular time. Draw a histogram to illustrate this data.

Before we can draw our histogram we need to add a further column (in green) to our table for frequency density. It can easily be calculated using:

$$\text{Frequency Density} = \frac{\text{Frequency of class interval}}{\text{Width of class interval}}$$

Age, A (Years)	Frequency	Frequency Density
0 ≤ T < 10	10	1
10 ≤ T < 20	20	2
20 ≤ T < 30	60	6
30 ≤ T < 40	50	5
40 ≤ T < 60	60	3
60 ≤ T < 100	20	0.5

We can now draw the histogram.

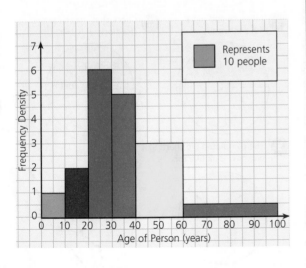

Scatter Diagrams

A scatter diagram is a graph which has two sets of data plotted on it at the same time. When plotted, the points may show a certain trend or correlation.

Positive Correlation
As one increases, the other also increases, e.g. number of ice creams sold and daytime temperature.

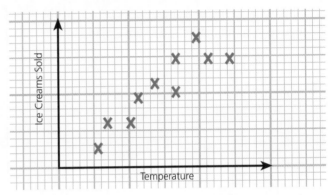

Negative Correlation
As one increases, the other decreases or vice versa, e.g. amount of petrol left in tank and distance travelled by car.

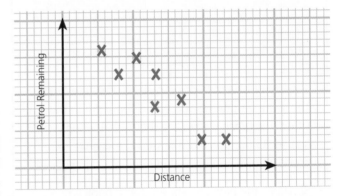

Zero Correlation
No obvious trend between the two, e.g. length of hair and height. Remember that zero correlation does not necessarily imply 'no relationship' but merely 'no linear relationship'.

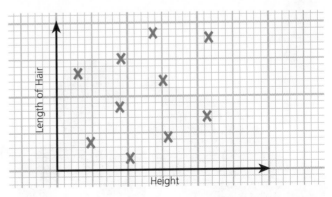

Displaying Data

Using a Line of Best Fit on a Scatter Diagram

A line of best fit can be used to estimate unknown values. This method is unreliable for providing estimates outside the range of values plotted.

Example

The diagram shows a strong positive correlation between some maths and science marks.

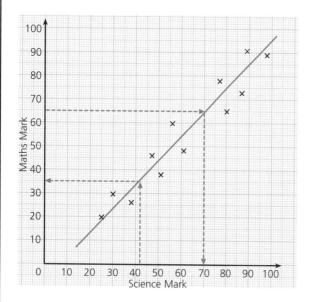

The line of best fit (red line) may be used to estimate the score on one test based on the score in the other. The green dotted line shows that a pupil who scored 65 in maths, but missed the science test, could be given an estimated mark of 70 in science.

Similarly, the blue line shows that a pupil who scored 42 in science could be given an estimated mark of 35 in maths.

Pie Charts

In a pie chart, the frequency for each class must be shown as a proportion. To draw a pie chart, we need to calculate the angle of the sector for each category.

Example

Favourite Sport	Frequency (no. of pupils)
Football	7
Tennis	3
Hockey	8
	Total = 18

Favourite Sport	Proportion of Pupils	Angle to be Drawn
Football	$\frac{7}{18}$	$\frac{7}{18} \times 360° = 140°$
Tennis	$\frac{3}{18}$	$\frac{3}{18} \times 360° = 60°$
Hockey	$\frac{8}{18}$	$\frac{8}{18} \times 360° = 160°$
		Total = 360°

Number who like hockey

Total number of pupils

1 Pick a starting point and draw a radius

2 Measure and mark 140° for football

3 Measure and mark 60° for tennis

4 Check that the remainder (for hockey) is 160°

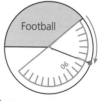

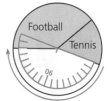

5 The completed pie chart will now look like this

Cumulative Frequency Diagrams

A cumulative frequency diagram usually produces an 's' shaped curve. It can be used to analyse the distribution of the data.

Example

The grouped frequency table alongside shows the time taken by 80 girls to travel to school on one particular day (to the nearest minute).

The cumulative frequency is the total frequency of that class interval, plus all the class intervals that precede it.

All points are plotted at the upper boundary of each class interval, e.g. (10,5), (20,14) etc.

Time Taken, T (minutes)	Frequency (i.e. no. of girls)	Cumulative Frequency
$0 < T \leqslant 10$	5	5
$10 < T \leqslant 20$	9	(9 + 5 =) 14
$20 < T \leqslant 30$	16	(16 + 14 =) 30
$30 < T \leqslant 40$	29	(29 + 30 =) 59
$40 < T \leqslant 50$	15	(15 + 59 =) 74
$50 < T \leqslant 60$	6	(6 + 74 =) 80

Once we have drawn the cumulative frequency diagram there are two ways we can compare the distribution of the data:

Median

The median is the middle value of our data. The median is obtained by drawing a line across (→) from half way up the cumulative frequency axis to the curve and then down (▼) to give its value. (In our graph this is at 40, i.e. $\frac{1}{2}$ of 80).

Interquartile Range

> Interquartile range = Upper quartile – Lower quartile

This gives us a measure of the spread of the data about the median. Two values are needed.

a) A line is drawn across (→) from three quarters of the way up the cumulative frequency axis and then down (▼). This value is called the upper quartile. (In the graph below this is at 60, i.e. $\frac{3}{4}$ of 80).

b) A line is drawn across (→) from one quarter of the way up the cumulative frequency axis and then down (▼). This value is called the lower quartile. (In the graph below this is at 20, i.e. $\frac{1}{4}$ of 80).

If we compare line ① at the bottom of our frequency curve with ②, we can see that a **box and whisker diagram** (or box plot) presents this more visually by differentiating between the interquartile range and the full range.

The method of displaying the median, quartiles and range is useful for comparing cumulative frequency graphs (as they all tend to have similar shapes).

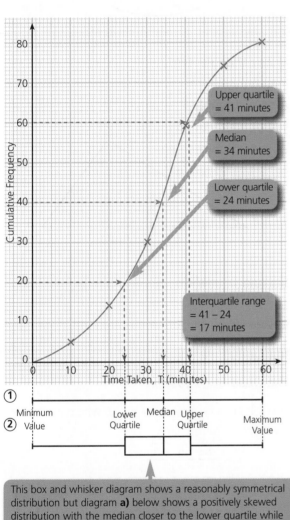

Upper quartile = 41 minutes

Median = 34 minutes

Lower quartile = 24 minutes

Interquartile range = 41 – 24 = 17 minutes

This box and whisker diagram shows a reasonably symmetrical distribution but diagram **a)** below shows a positively skewed distribution with the median closer to the lower quartile while **b)** shows a negative skew with the median closer to the upper quartile

a) 0 10 20 30 40 50 60 70 80 90 100

b) 0 10 20 30 40 50 60 70 80 90 100

Formulae Sheet

These are the formulae issued by Edexcel for higher tier students.

Area of a trapezium = $\frac{1}{2}(a + b)h$

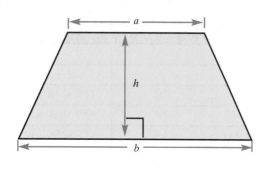

Volume of a prism = area of cross section x length

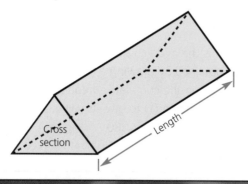

Volume of a sphere = $\frac{4}{3}\pi r^3$

Surface area of a sphere = $4\pi r^2$

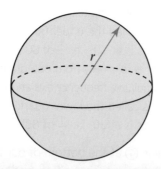

Volume of a cone = $\frac{1}{3}\pi r^2 h$

Curved surface area of a cone = πrl

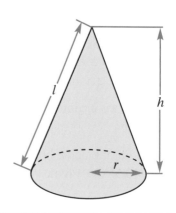

In any triangle ABC

Area of triangle = $\frac{1}{2}ab\sin C$

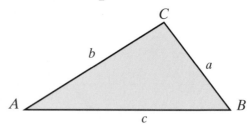

Sin rule: $\quad \dfrac{a}{\sin A} = \dfrac{b}{\sin B} = \dfrac{c}{\sin C}$

Cosine rule: $\quad a^2 + b^2 + c^2 - 2bc\cos A$

The Quadratic Equation

The solutions of $ax^2 + bx + c = 0$, where a ≠ 0, are given by

$$x = \frac{-b \pm \sqrt{b^2 - 4ac}}{2a}$$

Notes

Index